The Last Green Bottle

. . . in which Frank Hartley takes a last look round at the Sheffield he grew up in during the 1940's and 1950's.

Published in 1999 by Sheaf Publishing Ltd,
191 Upper Allen Street, Sheffield 3
ISBN 1 85048 019 2

Talking

I DON'T RECALL being over aware of my Sheffield accent as a kid. Only the way in which I chatted to other people in a perfectly understandable tongue, and that conversing amongst ourselves was never any problem.

It was a common idiom, shared by us all. One passed down from others already using it, as those before them had. So that we all knew perfectly well what we were saying, even if others struggled with it, or were too stuck up to learn. People such as our school teachers, carefully spoken types who wouldn't have been caught dead approving of such coarseness.

Mind you, I always put that loss on their part down to an occupational hazard. One of keeping up an appearance commensurate with their professional strata. Just like the doctor who examined us once a year,

The Wicker in the late 1950's, with proper tramcars, electric trains, an Austin A30 and room to drive them.

and old Mrs Tufnell on Weedon Street who charged five-bob an hour giving singing lessons to kids.

Christ knows how anybody could afford that then. I know we couldn't, and as for getting your money's worth . . . well. Put it this way, I never once heard of any of 'em going on to bigger musical things. Unless you count Betty Clithero's solo spot singing a song she wrote especially to perform before a full assembly for the Queen's engagement. And that was crap.

Even Mr Siddall – who played the piano for her – winced. But, as I said, they were the sort who turned up their noses at the likes of us. People who needed to sound posher to be different.

And where would we all be then, I ask?

Now it wasn't a case of us being simple, or even too naïve not to see our way of saying things were somewhat different to the other lot.

Simply that we, as a whole, preferred our own rudimentary Yorkshire made up of 'thee's and tha's'. Even though it may have driven a purist of English grammar to curl a lip at our deliverance.

A gesture that was futile, to be honest, for we actually enjoyed what was our heritage. It was a gift fashioned from harsh conditions prevalent in Sheffield even before the steel came; one developed and honed through earlier generations to become our own Sheffield dialect, embodying our Yorkshire roots, yet distancing our own particular part of it from from Rotherham, Barnsley and the rest. Our own little enclave, if you like, differing in sound to those of neighbouring areas no more than a good spit's length away.

So that, even to this day, anyone coming from Barnsley still sounds foreign to me. No . . . our's was better. It was un-sullied Sheffieldish, and we loved it.

Anyway, having I hope made those things clear, let me now state that despite their opposition to us there was never a time when I felt a grudge against anyone who would denigrate the way we talked, seeing such snobbery as being their problem, one that I would never allow to make me feel educationally sub-standard.

I may not have had the means to sound like those standing before the blackboard in class, but I certainly met their demands in reading and writing and the spelling of the words which their snobbery claimed that I pronounced all wrong.

A prejudice, I thought, and one that did not matter. Personally, I had no qualms about accepting my limited life style. Or the way in which it dictated the way I was taught to speak, and I totally rejected any bigoted suggestion that such restricted origins equalled a lack of intelligence.

A daft idea, I thought, perpetrated by the odd silly sod sent to teach us who suffered a class-conscious affliction; for had such balm pots given it a thought then sense might have told them that precise *manual* skills had made Sheffield famous.

Skills that had nowt to do with a perfect rendering of 'How now, brown cow', but were learned in a classroom of tradition and apprenticeship. Governed by older men who farted and cleared blocked noses with a thumb pressed against one nostril whilst violently blowing out through the other. Unconcerned about nicety, or where this obnoxious residue might land.

They were rough tutors, quick to clip the ear of a youth giving lip, or daft enough to think that shoddy work would do.

These were men who insisted on doing a job well, with pride in it, and were unimpressed by any fancy articulation of words you might care to parade.

For fancy words did not accurately read a micrometer. Did not grind smooth and clean a knife's bolster. Did not strip down the heavy plant of a rolling mill or charge a white-hot furnace.

Skill did.

'So get thi heead dahn anwatch arradothis'.

Such was our way of things, the natural criteria governing our perception of what was expected, the important things applicable to our industrial university. Yet, despite this order, nothing could stop me admiring the tonal quality of a beautifully modulated speaking voice.

Like the one displayed by Mr Popple, our metalwork teacher, rich and deep brown, soothing to hear and conjuring up for me a picture of the famous John Snagge who read out shipping forecasts on our wireless on the BBC Home Service.

It was a lovely sound, controlled and velvety as it told us of wind speeds, sea conditions and barometric fluctuations in an unhurried and calming way. Making you want for him to talk all night as his eagerly awaited bulletins went out. Calling to those sailing on dark forbidding seas, tossed in the frightening cauldron of a Force Eight gale. Firing my childish imagination with the magical names of distant places like Ross and Cromarty, Finnistere, Rockall, Dogger Bank, Outer Hebrides and Heligoland. And that mystical, fog-shrouded, place known only to ancient sailors as 'German Bight'.

His final wish of, 'Good sailing, gentlemen', stirs within me a love of being British even now, years later and long after he's gone.

But, John Snagge aside, I lost little sleep over envying anyone else in this matter of speech. I was happy instead to swan along with my mates 'dee-ing and dahr-ing' to our hearts' content. Living in this conversational bliss born of the accepted fact that our post-educational prospects would inevitably be manual.

Where nouns and adjectives added little to a pay packet reliant upon piece-work and bonus schemes. Following faithfully the grown-up advice which taught that happiness came only in the form of 'Shekels in thi pocket on Friday neet', advice that we blindly followed.

That's what I remember of it, because that's the way it was, through school and youthdom, wearing this vocal badge of implied manliness and sneering at the softness of those not sharing our way. Laughing at fussy mothers who forbade precious daughters from copying us lest it should brand them as being 'tarts'.

Creating a stigma which might lessen her family's hopes of marrying her off to some 'nice lad'. One who worked in an office or a bank, wearing a collar and tie beneath a hacking jacket sports coat, and politely said 'pardon', instead of 'tha what?' and backward enough to believe in all that tripe about 'saving it till we're married'.

A snobbish attitude, we thought, seeing such preference for that as being nowt more than blatant social priggishness on their part as well as an affront to their true class, their *Sheffieldish*.

Not to mention the frustrating smack in the gob it gave to any rampant sexual aspirations we might harbour towards such unobtainable beauties that we lusted over, dragging hard on Double Ace fags. With all of us not 'talking reight' and not comprehending why they should wish to be separate from us, from our lineage, and what we were proud of.

It will always be a time I remember as being eighteen years of selfish freedom. A time I would have been content never to change, except that change is inevitable in all things, and our way was no different in time's inexorable march. The war had finished and we all had jobs, bringing in good money for us to spend on things previously off limits.

Such as holidays taking in resorts far removed from our traditional east coast towns. Those working-class havens where everybody walking the promenade made it seem like home from home with their Sheffield talk. Hard working men on holiday who would brook no argument with any who sought to modify or change it. Happy to spend their time supping ale in seaside pubs on a two-week release from 'working neets dahn Vulcan Rooard'.

Then, with change, we stretched our wings to fly high and west to Torquay, or south to genteel Bournemouth. Unknown melting pots filled with a myriad of accents bearing little relation to our's.

Where 'Odda Oreight Kid?' was met by a puzzled stare or confused shrug, gaining for its purveyor a painful dig in his ribs from a wife or girlfriend anxious that strangers should not judge us to be common.

Women more concerned with appearance, hissing warnings into an unwelcoming ear, not realising that by such pressure did they chip away at our long-standing Sheffield identity.

Or there were young lads like me, called away to National Service. Taking us from those we knew to camps filled with those we didn't. Barbarians who were frivolous in their lack of intent to understand me, as I quickly learned by first experience of army life that October day in 1953. The day when, after a trying journey, I finally arrived at 3 Training Regiment in Catterick camp.

I recall vividly being utterly soaked to the skin, as well as feeling extremely cold, standing there before the main gate guardroom door. Still in an emotional spin from how everything had gone wrong on the journey up from Sheffield, I dreaded what lay in wait for me once I turned that waiting knob, and I recall clutching tightly under my armpit the decrepit little suitcase I'd brought, conscious that it was literally falling apart in its rain-sodden state

A disadvantage compounded by the discomfort being felt from a shoe whose welt had split, and leaked like a sieve, forming a soaking sock into a hard ridge shape that dug deeply along toes rubbed sore. A miserable way in which to arrive, especially two-and-a-half hours late, and not one that I would have chosen.

Not after all the months of building up to what should have heralded for me the start of a new life, one now no more than beyond that waiting door, a gateway I had eagerly discussed so many times with lads who had gone before me.

Mates I had grown up with who returned on short leaves to fill me with excitement over my own impending call-up. Fuelling a sense that craved to march with them behind a band and flags. Of being sent to foreign parts in a silly, film-induced euphoria of flushing out Japanese snipers still holding out in dark jungles. A new and exciting world, now no further away than the thickness of a door that I'd nervously tapped on and entered.

The sheer warmth of the place had embraced me within two steps inside, radiating out and away from a large round iron stove. A small metal front door in it open to show glowing red coke, a welcome I bathed in , so that, for a second, none of this strangeness mattered, or even existed. Only the warmth and the beaming smile coming to me from beneath the tall pipe reaching up and beyond the hut's roof. The first and solitary sign of friendliness I had encountered from leaving home that morning, albeit inanimate.

Not like the two men staring at me, cold of eye and silent, intimidating me with the presence of their uniforms.

One with two stripes, expertly whitened on sleeves

bearing razor like creases running from shoulder to cuff, standing by a side window, drinking hot tea from a brown enamel mug, sipping and watching me, with distant rows of Nissen huts showing beyond him through wet window panes.

The other bloke sitting behind a wooden trestle table, slumped forward with elbow bent, a hand supporting his bored-looking face, not bothering to change his pose whilst closely inspecting me, and obviously far from impressed by what he saw paraded in front of him. A Welshman, I later learned.

The two had won this opening gambit and they knew, no doubt having seen my sort of pallid fear many times before in the faces of countless new recruits. They knew that their uniforms and caps and polished boots were aces in a deck loaded to their advantage, and that the winning hand was in the way in which they knew the ropes when I didn't. Using their oppressive silence to increase the speed by which I was drawn into their web, knowing that eventually I would be the one to crack and ask for their help, as all those others had before me.

And had I but known it then I would have seen this for what it really was; my first lesson in Queen's Regulations, the one which taught that you must know your place. That should there be anything you felt you needed to know . . . you must ask. For as sure as hell no-one would offer it, as the cold gaze of those two glaringly proved.

So, I did what all those others had done. I cracked, and took the misguided gamble that apparent confidence might even the odds. Breathing deeply, I fished inside the soggy wet raincoat's inner pocket, a garment that had begun the day beige coloured but was now black with an overloaded weight of water, making its material reluctant to free the buff envelope I sought to flourish before them. The impressive one sent to me

Last sight of Sheffield as you left it by train in the 1950's – the Cosy Café opposite Midland Station.

bearing the embossed motif of Her Majesty's War Office.

It was my orders to report for service, borne safely with me all that way, orders they would have to read whether they liked me or not. Once I could manage to get the sodding things out of my wet pocket, that is. Succeeding only after a massive struggle, and passing them towards the seated one, I asked him, 'Candatellus worradoowidese?'

Words meant only to be a simple request for information, but I have to be honest and admit that they achieved absolutely nothing, a sign I took to indicate that I'd broken some rule of theirs and putting me even more on an edge. I then did what I thought to be the sensible thing. I spoke to them again, this time adding more content.

'Tintmafoltahmlait danose. Ampbinupeerafooa. Siledahnorlrooad, anall. Ampissedwethroo, siddee.'

Then, waving the envelope once again at the seated one, I'd asked, 'Duzdawandese? Orshallagiumim?'

Well, they could have been two of Burton's dummies for what good it did. Not being blessed with the mother tongue, they looked at me askance, and I was as baffled as they seemed to be, as well as feeling even more foolish than ever. Wondering if perhaps I'd slipped up by not calling him with the stripes 'sir', or that I'd failed to salute him. Or that the Welsh kid wasn't allowed to move until you said the correct password. In short, I simply didn't know.

So I'd quietly stood there, nervously watching as the both of them finally stopped looking at me and turned instead to look at each other. Him with the stripes gave Taffy boy an expansive shrug and said, 'What the frigging hell do you make of that, then?'

Years later, I can't blame them. When I see in print what I said then, even I have a job understanding it, and I've put a translation at the end of this chapter. But those words were simply my explanation of how the events of that day, along with the inclement weather and loss of direction had conspired to delay me. This I apologised for as I politely enquired as to which of them I should present my credentials.

The Welsh kid had slowly shook his head, answering in this deep voice which I immediately took a shine to, that he'd 'no idea, man. We've got sheep at home that make more sense to me. Is he English?'

And the striped one had shrugged again. 'If he is it must be a part we haven't frigging found yet. Where are you from lad?'

'Sheffuld.' I'd jumped.

'Oh... Sheffield, eh? And does everybody speak like that in Sheffield?'

'Aah,' I'd agreed.

'Aah?' Came his snap. Making me sway back in alarm.

'What the frigging hell is "aah"? You sound like one of his frigging sheep, lad. Say, "Yes corporal" when you speak to me... alright? You can manage that in English?'

'Coorsacan,' I'd blurted out.

'What?'

'Wotdateldus.'

'He's doing it again,' said the Welsh kid, rising to stand alongside his mate, who was now leaning over the table at me, shoving my offered envelope aside to put furious features inches from my face. An awful sight which in an instant reminded me of old Gus Fenwick back home whenever a Wigfalls collector caught him.

Close up, without touching me at all, yet driving me to momentarily blink in expectation of it. Just as I'd done in school, waiting for the cane to land.

'Stand yourself up frigging straight lad... NOW. You're sagging there like a withered TIT... Look at me, lad, not the floor... look at me and say, "Yes, corporal," ... right? Nothing else... just, "Yes, corporal"... GOT IT?'

'Yes, corporal,' I'd squeaked, through a tight throat, a pressing urge to run out filling me, giving way to relief as he'd pulled slightly back, perhaps convinced now that the pecking order between us had been established. But granting me only a moment's respite before once again renewing his verbal assault. This time it was a glaring, pointing and contemptuous attack at the way in which I wobbled before him, doing my utmost to balance aloft a rain-sodden foot still icy cold from a leaking shoe.

'Who the frigging hell told you to dance?... Eh? Put it down, lad... both together... NOW.'

'Meetewersersewer,' I'd whined, touching the toes down.

'What?'

'Shooslerrinwatterin... disoilinnit.'

'Jesus Christ.' He'd hit the roof. Snatching at my envelope to hit my head in time to his words, 'I cannot tell one frigging word you're saying, lad. In fact, I reckon you're taking the piss out of me. In which case I do not like you... not one bit.

'You... are late. You are also the ugliest little bastard I've seen today... including the RSM's frigging Pekinese.

'Now... I bet you think that you're Jack the lad... Eh? Well let me tell you this, you frigging alien. Any more of that gobble-de-gook and I will reach down your throat... seize your prune-like scrotum... pull it up inside your mouth... and frigging choke you with it. Right?'

And by now my head was nodding faster than me mother's sewing machine treddle when she'd got a rush on.

'Well then,' he'd roared in my face as a finale. 'Either speak English or piss off and join the frigging Navy'

It had not, I admit, been the best of starts, despite every conscious effort I had made to do everything right. I had not sought confrontation with anyone from leaving home, yet my day seemed to have been filled with obstacles and mistakes and a feeling of never again being able to do the right thing no matter how hard I might try.

A sense of injustice made me bitterly resent the bollocking as being uncalled for considering the way I had struggled to find them.

I mean, I'd gone through hell and high water just to join them. A scrawny little thing, wet through and doing my best to hold together a disintegrating case I'd given a bloke at work half-a-crown for.

And he'd robbed me, as I found out later, because it turned out to be one he'd used for years to carry maggots in when he went fishing.

Not that it mattered then, not with all this shouting and swearing coming my way, blooding me with the shock of it, even though I'd always known that sooner or later I would be on the receiving end.

My older mates had warned me of such things to come. Yet, never did I envisage such a ferocity of stinging words to be heaped upon me within the first five minutes of showing my petrified face.

I hadn't even got past the guardroom. Hadn't got through the gate nor told them my name yet. All I'd done was to try to apologise for being late and hand my papers in, and I finish up being made to feel responsible for the National Debt.

Anyway, the Taffy kid had re-seated himself, leaning back, hands behind head, and having a fair old smirk at my expense, doubtless enjoying my ordeal as a welcome break from the boring tedium of his daily routine in that warm hut.

And I found myself not liking him despite the earlier attraction of his different tongue. For that had now given way to a sense of anger for the pleasure he seemed to extract from my embarrassment, and I found myself longing to wipe that smirk from him by equally insulting his foreign sound to me. But I didn't.

I knew, even without experience, that such retaliation would not win me this day. That what was being dished out by the corporal had to be taken, like a foul dose of cod liver oil. That there would be no escape, and no going back to Sheffield until they said so. That once inside their camp there would not be anyone of my ilk waiting to give me a playful dig or the friendly comfort of 'Dalbee alreight, kid'

My welcoming committee was making those truths perfectly plain, right from Day One. You're in the army, now, lad, and here is where you start again. Where there's no going home sulking to mammy, and nobody 'dee's and dah's'.

Such, then, was my initiation. The umbilical cord

holding me to a recent past severed, entering me into a system which I had awaited and dreamed of from leaving school. One, hopefully, to take me on far journeys to parts of the Empire I had coloured red on world maps in an exercise book, or studied in enlargement hanging from classroom walls.

A chance to see and hear and smell the difference of foreign places at Her Majesty's behest and at no extra cost to myself.

That was what I told myself awaited me now, and all the trials or tribulations or insults inflicted upon me that first day of joining were to be no more than the entry fee I must pay to realise it. Of that I was determinedly sure.

In truth, I did not find an early adjustment to army life easy to make. But then, having only previously experienced a narrowly defined life it was to be expected, as others with me discovered, whatever their origin.

For we were a mixed bunch drawn from many diverse parts. Not like most of my childhood pals who had found themselves called into predominately Yorkshire regiments, gaining a benefit denied me in that their Sheffieldish did not isolate them in the Yorks and Lancs, the Duke of Wellington's, the Green Howerd's or the famous King's Own Yorkshire Light Infantry, who could march quicker than Ben Kettleborough's coal lorry could run.

No, their posting had none of my drawbacks. For they could establish a rapport with others of the White Rose, whilst I struggled with the accents of Cockneys and Cornishmen and Midlanders, not to mention the slight problem of trying to understand an upset Geordie or the nightmarish translation needed when a Glaswegian got seriously drunk.

An assortment of brogues which in retrospect I'm now glad I shared with my own. For National Service was indeed a broadening of my life, and that was what I searched for then, even though there were times in those first weeks when others sought to repeat the ridicule afforded me on that first day. But as time went on, my broad Sheffield accent gradually became less of an amusement to them. Except for one, and he duly paid for it.

I adjusted, learning to accept the fact that change can also demand sacrifice, and, loathe as I might be to part with it, concealing my pure Sheffieldish had to be done. For, with little doubt, it would have boded ill for me in the eyes of those painstakingly instructing me in the iron-clad procedures of correct transmission of messages via the air-waves had I finished off such properness with a cheery, 'Tha knows'.

So, I didn't. I did it their way, submerging that which in the past had comforted me with identity and replacing it with a manner demanded by my new masters. This was a victory for them never achieved by our school teachers, yet one that I did not deeply begrudge.

Sheffieldish had no place in Catterick, or any other part they might send me. It lay back home against smoking chimneys that cruelly dirtied lines of washing strung across a yard.

It lay with cloth-capped men playing crib and dominos in smoke-filled taprooms and jokey women conductoring on trams, back where I had begun, and sometimes felt homesick for.

I had now started anew, packing away carefully into the bottom of my brand new kit bag all of those 'Wossupwiddee's' and 'Wosdawiddeesen's'. Storing them for the day when once more I would return to where I first found them.

They were to be my talismen, the ones I would occasionally dust off to remind me of my roots. Bringing comfort, should I sometimes need it, by their 'Made in Sheffield' history, just as I was, by nature as well as tongue. My call-up time would be no more than a passing alteration to that fact, thrust upon me now by changed conditions, ones which I would have to accept in exchange for this wider experience now offered me, away from the smoke and the daily sameness of a young life.

Away from waiting for it all to begin, and the days of not talking reight.

* * * *

IT IS PERHAPS only fair to those not of our local tongue that I put the following meanings to words they might possibly have struggled to understand in this chapter.

Candatellus worradoowidese?
Would you please enlighten me in this matter?

Tintmafoltamlait, danose
I deny being responsible for not arriving on time.

Siledahnawlrooedup
The weather was damn wet throughout my trip.

Ampissedwethroo, siddee
Have you noticed my damp condition?

Duzdawnadese orshallagiumim?
Which of you two is better placed to accept my papers?

Wossupwidee?
Do you have a problem?

Wosdawisdeesen?
Were you un-accompainied at the time?

Coorsacan
But of course.

Wotdateldus

Two Penn'orth of Copper

I HADN'T SEEN little Ted Roberts since our schooldays together. Until one day back in the 'sixties when I called in the fish market for a mug of tea at that café stall which everyone seemed to use. To be honest, I didn't notice him standing alongside me at first, being more concerned with catching the eye of this sour-faced girl serving. Obviously doing her best to cope on her own. And what with several of us trying to order at the same time, I put her miserable look down to being fed up. So I didn't notice him.

Mind you, what with his severe lack of height, plus the nudges and knocks you got from the passing crowd

Well remembered by so many of my age is this entrance to the famous Sheaf Market at the bottom of Commercial Street, mindlessly destroyed by the City Council in the early 1970's.

as you stood there, it wasn't too surprising.

But I'm stood there, unaware of this kid that I haven't seen in ten or twelve years, when this row breaks out between the girl and an old fella standing a couple of yards away to my right.

Seems like she'd cut a bread-cake in two, smeared it with beef dripping, and served it up to him on one of those faded white plates of theirs. You know the sort, chips out of the edges and brown veins criss-crossing everywhere like a spider's web.

Anyway, she's served him on one and is demanding ninepence for it in the sort of no-nonsense tone that tram conductors used when the car was full and the last two on refuse to get off.

So, this old lad stands there gaping first at her, and then at this bread-cake. Obviously not in tune with her demands. And again, obviously, making no effort to pay for it either.

Now this hesitation on his part didn't quite fit in with the rather busy schedule that she was caught up in, a fact she made plain by again snapping at him for the money. Giving the plate yet another push across the counter towards him. And his response was to shove it back yet again, insisting that he hadn't ordered it. Mesmerising us all watching, as the plate shot back and forth between them like it was some sort of tennis with the rest of us there trying to keep up with the ball.

Until, no doubt fed up of this embarrassing encounter, the old lad had really lost his temper, saying that his request had been for a packet of pork scratchings and that if she couldn't get a simple order like that right she'd be 'better off serving crabs' all day.

Now that *did* make her think. Made her step back from him. Face noticeably reddening, and eyes flicking over the lot of us, she asked aloud for the potential owner to speak up, seeking a way out of this confrontation.

'It's mine,' had come this voice on the far side of the square stall. All eyes swivelled to take in this younger fella wearing a post office uniform. A half-smoked cigarette stuck in his mouth as he raised his head from inside the *Daily Herald* held out full stretch before him.

The confession had the old man positively glowing as the girl scampered across to deposit the plate where it really belonged, and quickly returning to place the pork scratchings packet before him. But instead, he bent to clasp the handles of his big leatherette shopping bag, straightening with the weight and turning to leave, in one movement.

'What about these?' she'd said, pointing to the packet.

And his answer was clear to us all. Loud and to the point.

'Shove 'em up thi' arse.'

And then he was gone. Swallowed up by the throng.

It was then that this voice alongside and below my shoulder spoke. Saying aloud how that old man's revenge had 'served her right . . . she's allus playing hell wi' customers'.

I'd felt inclined to turn and give a nod of agreement, having just witnessed it, then realising as I'd looked down that it had actually come from Ted Roberts, Tiny Ted. Or, as we always known him . . . Snuff.

Large as life, if you'll pardon the exaggeration, beside me. The Elf of Earsham Street. He was finishing off the last vestiges of a bacon and tomato dip sandwich, and judging by the shiny area covering the lower half of his face the dip had won the battle. He positively glistened with the stuff, although he made not the slightest effort to wipe himself clean as I looked down in surprise and delight at meeting him again.

All four-foot-ten of him, hardly looking a jot

different to the days before we lost touch on my call-up. Well . . . perhaps a couple of inches higher than then, but still well below my own average height.

A fact that, childishly I admit, did wonders for my ego. Just as it had before, when his little legs couldn't keep up with the rest of us.

For he was the smallest of us by far, forever condemned to bending his neck back to look at the face speaking to him. Save that is for babbies in prams, or those laying in bed. And, as in this later meeting, a habit he obviously still practised to that day.

Well, his mouth had shot open in the surprise of recognising me. A sight that I could have done without really seeing as it presented me with a distorted techni-coloured close-up of the mangled mess he'd been set to swallow. And then he'd spluttered a 'Hey up, Frank' through it, causing wet bits to fly my way. One of which attached itself to the soft area below my eye.

I forced a smile despite it, mentally noting not to flick it off whilst he was watching lest it should offend whatever sensitivity may be lurking behind his sloppy mouth. And I'd wondered to myself why it is that I let people do to me what I don't do to them in case I cause offence. Anyway . . . he recognised me, spat all over me, then spent the next minute ignoring me to concentrate on drinking his tea, making me wince at the horrendous noise he made cooling it before each sip.

It was one of those disgusting anti-social sounds which presents you with the problem of either laughing at it, condemning it for its barbarity, or fetching a market bobby to remove its source.

In plain language, it was awful to hear. Very much like the sickening 'thwok' sound you get when dragging your welly out of deep clinging mud.

Still, that aside, we'd got to chatting about things past. And I'd recalled that the last remembered time of seeing him was the night our gang came across him standing outside of the Union Street *Picture Palace*.

Our gang had been on our way to see a double bill at the *Empire Theatre* on Charles Street at the time. Joe Loss and his Big Band Show, coupled with Norman Evans, who at that time was one of our big comics.

He'd come on dressed like a middle-aged harridan complete with turban and wrap over pinafore to match what appeared to be a toothless mouth. Then he'd lean over this prop garden wall, standing behind it on a box, and go into this funny routine of what everyone else in their street was up to. Until, right on cue, the box would give way, crashing him down to squash this huge false bosom he wore and continually pushed around to find comfort in.

Hilariously grimacing with a grotesque expression at the pain of it, declaring with a gasp that it was the, 'Third time this week I've done that . . . and it's always on the same brick'

Anyway, like I said, we're heading for a laugh with good old Norman when we spot Snuff. And he's standing with this lass who towered over him even without the help of the piled-up hair-do that's she's sporting, while he's got this expression I can only describe as looking like a poodle dog fancying a Great Dane.

Now, when I remarked earlier about how small he was that day years later in the fish market, well . . . that was positively tall to how high he stood that night in town. Despite his efforts to conceal the truth by developing this unusual gait whereby, to give the impression of being taller, he literally tottered about on his toe ends.

Now, without a doubt his height, or lack of it, had plagued him from birth. In fact his brother Wilf told us that up to being four years old, Tiny Ted could easily hide behind a cushion. And his mam would think the mite was playing in the street. I do know that twice she had us roaming after dark shouting for him, thinking he'd wandered off and fearing the canal. And both times he'd turned up safe at home.

Anyhow . . . there he is that night in town with this bored-looking bird pretending not to see us due to the cashier in the pay box refusing to let him in because it was an 'A' picture. And he didn't look anywhere near sixteen, which you had to be then to get in on your own. Unless it was a 'U' certificate film like Abbott and Costello. A rigid system which led to millions of kids my age standing outside cinemas in all weathers, pleading with anyone old enough to 'Tek one in please mester . . . or missus' depending on the gender.

But you see, sadly, Snuff *was* sixteen, even though he could pass for a nine-year-old choir boy. And, to compound the embarrassment to his love education, this officious ticket-selling sod had mistaken this bird for being Snuff's big sister. Now this was an assumption she'd resented, especially as in the ensuing exchange the cashier had the further gall to suggest that she should be ashamed of herself for bringing a little lad like him to the second house showing. Especially up town . . . and after dark at that. Comments poor little Snuff could have well done without, seeing his hopes of a back row wrestling bout with this bint he'd brought get no further than the front of the queue.

Yet, the assessment of his age that night was understandable, even though it did leave his date disgusted at the outcome after giving in to his repeated pleas for her company.

Circumstances which, due to our arrival on the scene, had created the perfect hunting conditions for that well-known Attercliffe barracuda Harry Owen. A natural predator of anything that had no need to shave. And one who, at the faintest trace of female scent, could make a bloodhound look like it was riddled with hay fever. His own mother once described him as having the ways of a 'lodging house tom cat' . . . and she loved him.

So it surprised us not that poor little Snuff's demise at entertaining this lass was Harry's chance to live up to his nickname of Jack Flash. And true to that, he had her back in the queue before she had time to learn his name. Blatantly feeling at her bum all the way down the line and grinning back at us over his shoulder, contemptuously immune to the anguished look of the little lad who'd brought her. As well as our envy at what he was feeling at.

Take it from me, the round of 'effs' Snuff gave the pair of 'em that night made several older men nearby give him threatening glares. My last sight of this midget was one of a sad little figure trooping off, head down and hands thrust deep inside the pockets of long trousers which had been reduced by nine inches, disconsolate at the thought of Dirty Harry enjoying the soft rewards of the bus fare he'd invested in the treacherous tart.

Actually, Harry did reveal to us later how relieved the girl had been when he'd whisked her away. This was in part to the embarrassing refusal of entry in front of everybody queuing to get in. And to how conspicuous she'd felt at Snuff's insistence of her putting her arm through his as they'd made their way through town, especially as she'd had to reach down to do it. Add to all of this the elf-like features of her beau and there's little doubt that her high expectations of watching Ava Gardner in *Mogambo* that night were somewhat less than the poor little sod who'd offered to pay for her. And, upon hearing this I felt glad for him. Glad that Harry had purloined her from him.

For knowing of his capacity in such matters, I was sure that there would have been large parts of the film that she was bound to have missed.

I confidently base this on the running commentary given to us once by fat Peggy who worked in Woolworth's down the 'Cliffe on the counter selling rubber heels and shoe leather.

Now she'd let Harry take her to the *News Theatre* in Fitzalan Square one time, and according to her report she only managed to see the half of one cartoon and a bit of Gaumont British News, despite being in there over two hours. I reckoned that Snuff could take comfort in knowing that the one he'd lost would have most probably spent far more time surveying the ceiling than drooling over the famous film star she was desperate to see.

The memory of all this re-emerged that day I met him again years later. Not that I cared to remind him, seeing no sense in wanting to stir the pain of it for him once more.

So I'd spoken of other things, pertinent to that magic time we'd shared in short trousers, forever dreaming of long ones. Trying my best to suppress the laugh I'd felt within at the fact, that despite him being now into his manhood his overall height had hardly increased from the time I'd left to join the Forces.

Anyway . . . we'd chatted away. And I learned that unlike my own progress which had been pretty straightforward from leaving school, Snuff's had been more varied.

Mind you, things could be then.

You could 'jack' a job in during the morning, visit the Labour Exchange at dinner time, and be earning a wage working for somebody else that afternoon.

No sweat. It was so easy that all the big works had notice boards at their main gates listing dozens of vacancies on offer, skilled or not. Blue or white collar. It mattered not as employers cried out for our labour to meet the demands of order books, struggling to fulfil promises to all corners of this land. And beyond.

Halcyon working days of wages each week. Bumped up by guaranteed overtime or bonus which gave all of us leaving school a kaleidoscope of choice as you took that first uncertain step into a grown-up world, where men worked eight-, twelve- and even sixteen-hour shifts and came home on Friday with loadsamoney. And plenty more of it next week.

They dedicated their hours to the swelling of a wage packet, filled to over-flowing by the Lord God of Labour who beamed down upon them from above the shower of pound notes he dropped. So that time spent with their kids would be brief, a slot fitted in between time earmarked for shift-work and the ale house.

Fathers were shadowy figures who went to bed from nights before you got up, and left again whilst you were out playing after school. Figures that owned you without their presence, except on the occasion when your mother decided that you deserved the strap.

Men who made up for their absence at work by once a year taking their families for a caravan holiday at Ingoldmels or Humberston Fitties, booked straight after Christmas or you didn't get in.

Occasionally splashing out to afford proper digs in boarding houses in Skegness or Bridlington, houses which chucked you out at ten in the morning despite it pissing down with rain. Thousands, like lost sheep in pac-a-macs, feeding endless pennies into early-day fruit machines. Whilst mam and dad sat in seaside pubs comparing the meals they were being served at night with somebody else who was getting better.

'Salmon? Yore got salmon last neet? Bleeding hell . . . we got corn beef pie . . . wheer did tha say yore stopping?' And yet, despite such complaints, you'd still feel superior to those struggling to carry water cans to a stand pipe six times a day whilst holidaying in caravans lit by fragile gas mantles that crumbled to the touch of a wayward match. Slipping and sliding on the rain-soaked site to reach toilet blocks with concrete floors awash from some sodding kid who'd deliberately left a tap running for spite, perhaps in revenge for being given the regular job of crawling beneath his 'van to bring out that greasy slimy galvanised slop bucket you had to empty everytime your mother washed up.

Don't you just miss it?

Like hell I do. And I'll crown the barmy chuff who says that holidays aren't the same anymore.

Still . . . let's get back to Snuff Roberts. And how fate decreed that he'd never reach a light switch without standing on a stool.

Starting with the nickname he brought with him the first time his mum dumped him outside of our school gates. Calling him by it as she went through the lecture all mothers delivered to their kids on that big day in their life. Warning about 'being good'. And how 'Billy Swift is in your class so sit wi' him . . . and mek sure nobody pinchs thi cooat'.

Anyhow, it turns out that his own dad first called it him when, at a very young age, tiny Ted decided one day to break the monotony of clipping his mam's pegs together by inserting up his nose this small pearl button he found in the bottom of her peg bag. He no doubt instantly regretted this experiment when his failure to retrieve it resulted in the painful retribution of his panic-stricken mother trying to do it for him and failing, what with her finger being twice the size of the hiding place so she'd just about shook his brains out by yanking him upside down, violently encouraging the thing to leave.

Especially seeing as it was one of a set she'd lost after cadging them from an elderly aunt to sew down the front of her best silk blouse.

Anyway . . . getting nowhere with this rather crude approach, and with Ted's face now purple from the blood rushing to it, she'd whipped him the right way up and set off at a gallop to find his dad.

With him, as usual, comfortably ensconced in the *Sportsman* pub for his usual dinnertime bevvy, and no doubt wondering what somebody had put in his beer, when their old lass barged in. Clutching his youngest offspring horizontally upside down under one arm as it yelled the place down. An interruption not really appreciated at a time when he was mentally locked in the problem of whether to play his double two or not in a crucial game of dominoes called 'five and threes'.

It was clearly an entrance to cause a stir, further emphasised by her bouncing the kid down on the table before him, sending the black and white ivories zooming all over the place, and causing much sadness amongst the four lovingly playing the game. No doubt, and understandably, they were somewhat peeved at how the whole ambience of the contest had been rudely marred. Especially Ted's father's two opponents, who only needed four more holes on the crib board to win a free pint from him and his partner.

Now . . . bearing this in mind, you will understand why a big fuss was not made of the boy, despite his predicament. A re-action which was conveyed by way of glares and much muttering about 'bleeding pudding burners bringing kids in here'. Ill-mannered remarks which drove the husband to seek a way to placate them by riling on at Ted's mother for an explanation of this invasion of his privacy, and using his best working class diplomacy at one point to demand her reasons for making him look a 'reight twat' in front of his mates.

He rounded it off with more pleasantries of a similar vein which, when sifted, amounted to a rebuke over the way she'd failed to stop the lad from being so inventive in his play, or, as he put it, 'Tha should spend less time warming thi arse and more time watching him'.

All this amid volumes of woodbine smoke, and surrounded by pint-swilling steelworkers. Then up steps big Hilda Whitely, pushing aloft her bulk from her seat beneath the filthy window. The one with the faintly discernible *Gilmour's Ale* printed on it. One which hadn't seen a leather across it since Armistice Day in 1919.

'Shift,' she'd said. And they all did. Sharply.

You didn't argue with Hilda, on account of her being built like a four-ton press, as well as a countenance which convinced us kids that we must have done summat wrong if she looked at us. A fierce woman commanding a lot of respect, she was often called upon by other women to perform that time-honoured necessity in those days of 'laying out' the corpses of loved ones departed. She prepared them for their final journey with a gentleness that belied her bulk.

Yet, amusingly, because of her size she was also often the antidote used whenever some young bull got out of order from the drink and was asked to leave the pub she used. For whereas he might use violence on any man, he was made powerless by humiliation as he was bodily bumped through the door by big H's ample belly.

As I said, she was quite a girl to have around. And many a lad wished he'd got drunk elsewhere.

Anyway . . . up steps Hilda. Barging others aside and fishing from her pocket that familiar round silver coloured 'Top Mill' snuff tin. The one she took everywhere, even when she was struggling to get the shoes on a 'stiff' whose feet wouldn't bend,

In fact, I bet they were odd times with an awkward one when she'd said 'sod it' and broke off for a quick sniff, a pleasure that might have killed her with shock had one of her comatose clients shot up and asked to

share before they screwed on the lid.

Not that they'd have necessarily got one, mind you. For the sharing of this fine ground tobacco dust was indeed a mason-like procedure, one to be followed before you'd be offered the honour, where the bearing of the true trademarks showed you to be a believer. Signs like the brown staining beneath the nose, and the fall-out stripes that marked your coat lapel or waistcoat front. The grooves formed in a finger and thumb by pressing tightly upon the edge of a button, creating a clandestine storage space that allowed extra to be taken up when plunged into an offered tin. Your unsuspecting benefactor unaware of the scam as, smiling through the robbery, he followed tradition using the opening gambit in this ritual.

'Would tha like a bit up?'

To which the thieving rascal taking his liberty would cheekily riposte.

'Go on then . . . just a pinch.'

Attercliffe Common at the corner of Broughton Lane in the late 1960's, showing the grim reality of this area even in a time of full employment.

As they used to say then. There are real people ... and then there are Christians.

Personally my sole contact with this habit was in the early days of my smoking career, via one of the wet grinders I met in the cutlery trade.

I'd be fifteen then, and he showed me the easy way of inducing yourself into it by dipping the end of your fag in some before lighting it.

And I can tell you that it made a marked difference to the usual feel of smoke going down your throat. Smoother, with the feeling of a clearing sensation in your lungs as it went down. Feeling much cleaner than the normal tightness brought on by the weed.

It was a sensation I actually enjoyed and felt better for. And although I never got around to buying it myself, one that I never refused on the rare occasion it was offered.

I can't remember that grinder's name now, but I clearly recall the sight of him doing his trade, one that separated his kind from the rest of us as we all strove to match Sheffield's finest.

And I think back to his terrible job. Sitting in a wooden saddle atop this terrifyingly large grinding wheel whirling beneath him for twelve hours a day.

Driven by slapping leather belts that dropped from a giant spindle spinning above his bent head and shoulders. Subject to a curtain of cold water spraying up over him from a trough which these dangerous spheres skimmed. An icy lubricant providing that vital wetness across the wheel's width, which prevented the black blades which these men skilfully ground from scorch marks as the crude scale was driven off, leaving a bright finish for the rest of us to glaze, polish and whet to an expected brilliance.

Superb items of fashioned steel to grace fine tables. Born of men like him who invariably ended their working lives with hands gnarled and wracked by rheumatism. Wrinkled by the water that went with it and the legacy of fingers crooked from years of gripping the wet template which held the dark blanks which fed the spinning wheel that ruled their lives.

Memories which evoke a wry smile from me when an outsider in their ignorance of such things praises our past renown. Had they, as I did, witnessed the reality of that industry forty or more years ago, perhaps their pride in our local history would be tinged by the same unease that I felt then over the limelight which others earned for us.

But that's another tale.

So, as I was saying, Big H pulls out her snuff and telling the mother to hold him still, runs a line of it down the back of her hand. Clamping the young Snuff's face with her free hand, she sticks the powdered one under his nose and blows.

WHAM . . . his head shot back. His eyes doubled in size. His tongue shot out and his face went into orbit. His infant mind was obviously in turmoil trying to cope with this barbaric irritant making his nose tingle and burn.

Leading him into stage two of the drama where his breathing became a series of rapid intakes, tears forming in saucer-like eyes as this usual process followed its natural course. Until . . . WHOOSH.

And the birth of all this to-do came rushing from him like a silver-coloured Excocet, threading laser-like between those watching, to land with a melodious 'plop' in the surface of a half-finished pint clutched by a man at the back, whose features changed from surprise to distaste, demonstrating that despite a forty year love affair with the fluid it didn't stretch to ignoring a snot-covered button on the bottom.

But, the method worked. And another nickname was

added to our substantial list. One he would take into school and beyond.

One that, by inference, seemed to accentuate his smallness, giving the rest of us a reason to gloat, an opportunity to stress our own good fortune in inches.

And it brings back an image of him then, in the growing years, as a short-trousered miniature, forever trailing the rear of us in our street wanderings.

He was a 'tick', a shadow forever hovering over our perimeter whenever the gang formed, talking, laughing, and larking beneath pale gaslight.

Leaving him ignored or ridiculed with the occasional clip if he dared to join in with us. As you do in your ignorance as kids, when prejudice feeds the fallacy which says that what you see is the sum total of it all.

As we did to little Ted Roberts.

Until the day when he and a lass were picked to represent our school in a massed choir, made up from many others around the city, to sing with the Hallé Orchestra in concert at the City Hall. On a grand scale. In a setting that overwhelmed me as I sat with the multitude above it, lost in the awe that it generated, even before the Hall filled.

For here lay something beyond my ken. A savoury feast of clear music made up of highs and lows formed by golden instruments that threw out sparkling light shafts by their movement.

Of this black-coated man standing above the others, arms flailing and bringing forth deep booms of percussion out of giant copper clad drums. Making your breath pause at the realisation that such resonance draws and feeds upon the beat which it exerts. Causing me to await nervously its next explosion.

Yet not letting it distract me from scanning the massed ensemble of scrubbed kids on stage, forming their tiered semi-circle above and around those producing this music, which I couldn't profess to understand, but which had me riveted by its presence and effect.

A complexity of colour and consuming sound produced to order by the secret sign language spoken by the magic hands of John Barbirolli. Coaxing, commanding, groaning and silencing them at his will. Imperiously watched over by those majestic stone lions, silently and unmovingly guarding him.

And I recall the nervous stillness we'd felt, caught up in this shared experience designed to show us that life needn't consist of just muck and labour, and noting how many took refuge from this enlightenment by way of giggles and whispers.

But others, like me, welcomed this scene that flooded our senses, filling the void created by ignorance with respectful silence. Drinking it in with a jealous desire to be a part of it. To be down there on that lion-protected stage with little Snuff, wherever his insignificant frame may be.

Realising with a shock how wrong we had been to judge him by size. That he had fooled us. And I wanted to take his place.

We'd talked of him afterwards, in the long queue we formed on Fargate for the tram ride back. Marshalled by irritated teachers who slapped the heads of those pushing their luck. Quickly forgetting the peace generated in the dying notes of *Greensleeves* as the real world returned. Snapping in their annoyance at our chatter, not recognising it as the relief felt by many at being once more inside familiar boundaries of behaviour.

Re-asserting that resistance to being impressed by an art form not fashioned by muscle or machine, lest it be seen as a sign of weakness and non-manliness. Accepting once again the restriction on being an individual which comes with fitting in. Finding comfort in their chat.

'Did tha see him banging dem big cymbals,' someone chortled, puffing out cheeks and belly in a parody of the portly orchestral player in question. Drawing our laughs at him as we donkey-nodded.

'Ah wondered wheer our bin lids were,' he'd continued. Eager to keep the limelight we'd allowed him. 'We cud do wi' dem at hooam . . . me fadder'd never be late on mornings.'

We preferred the answer given him by another, who'd said in heavy sarcasm that, 'da wunt get dem in yore 'ouse . . . not wi all dem kids wot yor've got . . . me mam sez yore old fella must 'ave been crossed wi' a rabbit'.

The first joker reddened in anger and embarrassment, scowling at the laughter now turned against him. Somehow feeling a shared guilt over his father's vigorous habit.

And it struck me then how shallow and brief the lad's glory had been when compared as a bed mate to the experience that day of little Snuff.

An impression rekindled once more when we talked of it that day years later. Swathed in the sounds and smells and wetness which the fish market generates.

But he'd remembered, and expressed surprise that I could recall a day that should have been more of a highlight to him than me. Jerking his head back in a gesture which said it all when I confessed that, no matter how hard I'd tried, I hadn't been able to see him amongst that illustrious host.

'Tha wunt 'ave,' he'd sniffed. 'They stuck us reight behind one o' dem lions so ah never saw owt meesen either . . . only thing I remember is this lass behind me who pissed hersen . . . and we were all trying not to stand in it.'

And I'd spluttered into my tea in laughter at this. The unfairness of it all, that fate should give this harmless dwarf a place in the pageant and then stick him out of our view behind a posing beast that cared little for his vocal efforts. Whilst I, out there in the crowd, envied him his place.

He'd half smiled at it, shrugging off my poorly hidden amusement of it all.

'Story of me life, innit,' he'd sighed, before quickly rejecting my effort to soothe the disaster by saying there'd been plenty of good times to make up for it. Pointing out to me instead how his lack of inches had always been a handicap that we had used against him.

Like the night we'd banged on a door before doing a runner, oblivious to his lack of our pace as we'd hared away. Only this time, unknown to us, the victim of the prank was being visited by her big son. And he just happened to be a Yorkshire Harrier. A bloody good un and all.

'Cos he'd caught Snuff inside of twenty yards, lifting him on high by the scruff of his neck as his little legs kept running. Even in mid-air.

And I can still hear the yelps and squeals he'd made when we stopped to listen to the summary punishment being administered, leaving the rest of us mightily relieved that *he* was the one getting it.

But then, he was used to good hidings, having taken them on a regular basis from his drunken slob of a dad. A point I'd borne in mind as we chatted, pressing him to fill in the gaps from leaving school. And the rolling events he'd unfurled had me almost thanking God aloud that I hadn't been born him.

Honestly, I was stuck as to what I should do; laugh or pat him on the head in sympathy. Especially as he never once let slip that hang-dog expression of resignation. Daft as it sounds, and despite his tale of

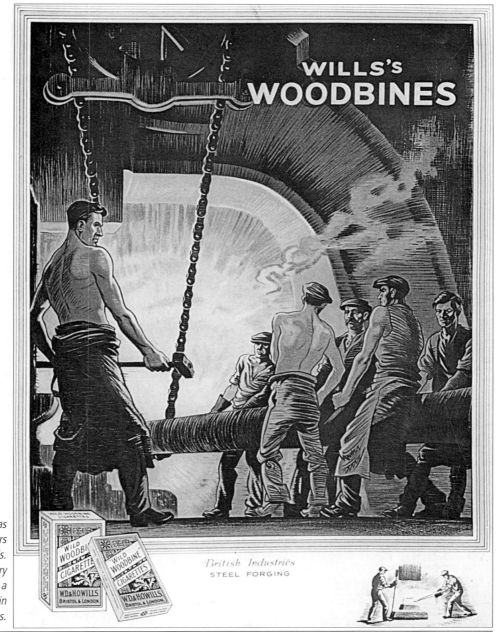

Working Sheffield, as seen by the advertisers in the 1940's. Woodbines were very popular, and quite a cheap cigarette in those days.

woe, he brightened my day for me, raising that familiar desire that makes me mentally file away such events for future reference. The kind I like to dust off and air whenever I'm in good company and having a pint. Talking over the old days. People like Snuff, who at this part of the proceedings was busy ladling five spoonfuls of sugar into the fresh mug of tea he'd just demanded from the sour-faced assistant. A liberty she obviously disapproved of, judging by her glare as she crudely snatched the basin away, banging it down again further along the counter.

This manoeuvre brought a curt, 'miserable cow,' from our lad as he somehow managed to sip this syrup and scowl back at her at the same time.

'So,' I'd said, wincing at the noise being made. 'Are tha working?'

He'd shook his head at that, looking away, giving me a feeling that I shouldn't have asked. So I'd hastily tried to repair the damage, asking over his parents, trying my best to make a joke of the capacity his dad had showed for mopping the ale, and getting in return a resentful look for my trouble. The mention of the man plainly affecting him.

'Aah,' he'd said, bitterly. 'He cud mop ale alreight . . . all our family's got scars to prove it'.

I nodded, knowing this to be true from the marks he'd bore when he'd played with us.

So I'd asked, not wanting to appear too interested, if Snuff still saw him.

'Not since ah were fourteen. We all left him . . . went to live wi' me grand-dad at Neepsend . . . ah was glad an' all . . . me and our kid used to climb on top o' wardrobe when he were pissed . . . he were a waster.'

It was my turn to look away, leaving him to slurp the tea in peace for a minute. Letting his anger at the memory subside.

And I'd changed tack, telling him of how I'd recently met our old mate Pete Fairfax. Of how he'd informed me that Snuff had left school to join a racing stable near to Pontefract. Over the moon at the apprenticeship and on course to be a famous jockey.

He'd made me wait for his answer, one hand in a trouser pocket and one leg over the other resting toe-down on the floor, doing his utmost to appear nonchalant as he leaned to brace himself one-handed against the counter's edge. Yet not having the height to make the effort effective.

'Got enny smokes?' he'd snapped at the serving girl as she passed once again. He scowled at her for ignoring him, making me uncomfortable at the obvious hostility between them.

'Only stuck it a month,' he'd muttered. Still glaring at her as he'd answered me. To which, light-heartedly, I'd pointed out that he'd hardly done himself justice, that dedication and a few years of learning his craft had to be accepted if fame and fortune were to be found. That such a small time hardly gave him the chance to distinguish one end of a horse from the other.

'Tha'rt joking,' he'd spat, 'That's one thing ah did learn, 'cos ah did nowt else but shovel shit . . . six in a morning while eight at neet . . . shovelling shit . . . tha's never seen as much shit in thi life . . . it were o'er me head . . . and when ah'd cleaned one stable out they gev me another to go at . . . wi' another dollop o' shit in it. Ah'm telling thi . . . ah cud 'ave stopped at hooam and got a job at Blackburn Meadows doing that . . . and got four times the money.'

Well, I'd looked away by now. Putting my mug of tea to my mouth to strangle the laugh at this tirade.

'Thirty-five bob a week ah got. Nowt to eat . . . no time off . . . up at half-past-four in a morning and a reight bollocking everytime he caught me sat down . . .

no kidding . . . ah used to fall asleep still holding that garden fork . . . and stink? First time they let me hooam me mother burnt all me clewers.'

Now what with him being generous with the decibels and as you might well imagine, all this was making the pair of us rather conspicuous.

Which was hardly surprising when you consider that his insistence on calling equine waste 'shit' wasn't doing a great deal towards enhancing the taste of fried butties being eaten all around us. In fact, two customers threw theirs down in disgust to glower at me before stalking off.

Consequently, in the interest of good taste, I'd acted sharply to change the subject. Telling him of my recent de-mob from the Army. Receiving in return yet another silent scowl as he began to vigorously rummage through his jacket's inside pocket, finally pulling forth this dented *Golden Flake* tobacco tin. Gingerly unscrewing the lid to reveal the tangled web of shredded strands used by so many then to roll their own fags.

That was an art I could never master, and watching the ease with which he expertly combined that paper slip with the ingredients of the tin to produce this match-thin cigarette, one that I never will.

Mind you, seeing the finished article, it all seemed a ridiculous waste of time to me. No word of a lie, but the first inch of it was nothing but an empty paper tube, totally devoid of any substance or life.

And when he stuck the thing in his month and rolled it around for a bit . . . well. It looked for all the world as though he was sucking a tapeworm.

But by far the best bit of all this was when he lit the thing. Because the whole of it just combusted itself into a torch, sending up a flame that just about enveloped one side of his face.

Not that this alarmed him too much. Because, apart from a brief backward jerk of his head from the heat of it, his only other response was to pluck the thing from his lips, blow hard upon its end to aid the ignition of those strands now smouldering, then jam it back in again.

'Wheer di tha learn to roll thi' own, Snuff?' I'd asked, impressed without wanting to emulate his efforts. Fighting not to laugh again at the sight of his hollow cheeks formed by these huge drags he was inflicting upon his creation to stop it dying the death.

'Borstal,' came the shock reply. Not caring to look at me in his confession of this boys' prison that at that time was enough to frighten us into good behaviour.

'Borstal? Tha's been to Borstal?' I'd gasped, part of me somehow excited by it all, even envious of the effect it had on others when you could claim knowledge of its insides.

I'd asked him how long he'd served and, with no sign of glorying in it, he'd told me six weeks. For breaking into a Co-op.

This staggered me. I mean, I'd got up to some daft tricks as a kid but the worst I'd ever copped for was a good hiding.

Six weeks in Borstal for getting caught, even in those much stricter times, seemed harsh to me. And I'd said so to him. 'Not when it's yer eighth time,' he'd shrugged, clearly unimpressed by the example of it, suggesting that he had known worse.

Gradually it unfolded that this sharp episode in his young life had followed on from his failed attempt to put the wind up Gordon Richards in the world of racing. As Snuff told it, his mam, whose married life had been far from blessed with happiness, had viewed her son's rather smelly return with a minimum of joy. She'd seen it as a God-given chance of making his name. And, I suspect, the advantage over other proud mothers who shouted the odds over their offsprings' progress in the more technical or practical apprenticeships of life.

Anyway . . . Snuff didn't return home, but turned his back on a system he saw as no more than an extension to the brutal, drink-soaked bullying of his father, a man whose first remark into his wife's sweat-dried face as he'd sullenly viewed for the first time this just-born minuscule addition to his brood, was the cutting sneer of, 'Ah thought ah told thee ah wanted a lad this time'.

Not surprisingly Snuff had responded to his grandfather. A more gentle and intelligent sort who filled and fired the lad with stories of his own life.

Of how, as a boy himself, he'd run away to work on a canal boat, ferrying coal from the pits of Yorkshire and Nottinghamshire destined for the avaricious furnaces of Sheffield and Rotherham.

Filling in the void of no formal education with a rich mixture of healthy hard work and the earthy normality of barge people and colliers and steelmen. A free wandering life of sweet smelling fields beside quiet waters, balanced by the ugliness of black industry.

This was a life young Snuff could shut his eyes and live as the old voice painted it for him. One he was convinced would have made him grow tall and strong, lifting him above those who never let him forget his size. This belief swelled with the faded photographs he was shown of the old man as a boy in khaki. No bigger than him and wearing a military cap at a rakish angle so that it appeared on the point of falling from the baby-like face that it swamped.

A smiling face. Alive with the excitement of war. One that was eager to be a hero. Supplementing this bygone image with stirring tales of machine- gunning Turks and Germans in the ancient land of Mesopotamia, making Snuff ache with the envy of what he'd missed, driving him to find that excitement by scaling Co-op walls after dark. Going on missions behind enemy lines. Returning with the spoils of war . . . until he was captured and paid the price of imagination.

By now I was at a loss, totally held as all this came pouring out. I hadn't expected it, my only intention being to generally enquire after so long without seeing him.

Obviously I had unwittingly triggered off this urge for him to unload these things that had deeply affected him. I was out on a limb that I hadn't sought, and I'd felt trapped by it, seeking a way out by asking if he'd followed the rest of us into National Service.

'Nah . . . failed me medical,' he'd said, with another shrug.

'Failed?'

'Ahh . . . failed. Put me down as 3C . . . said ah were too underweight for 'em . . . turned me down.'

I was back in a corner again. Embarrassed and this time almost desperate for something to say which wouldn't rebound. So I had copied his habitual shrug, lying that he hadn't missed out really. Making a poor joke of how I hadn't 'shot any Germans, either'.

Insisting it had all been 'bullshit and shouting' and that I'd counted the days off to getting out. But he had looked up scathingly at me, not believing a word. Hitting me again by saying that *I* hadn't been rejected. Adding, 'Thaa went . . . dint tha? Yer all went what ah knocked abaht wi . . . ah were only one not to go . . . and it weren't me weight tha knows . . . it were Borstal wot did it . . . they knew I'd got form . . . ah wanted to go and all . . . wanted to go abroad like yore lot did . . . know what I mean?'

It now seemed to me that every attempt to lift his gloom was a useless exercise. And a compulsion to rid myself of him and his problems swelled. I now badly wanted to leave, to dump him. Yet I couldn't find the heart to be callous enough to walk away without appearing uncaring.

I needed a way of showing that I was on his side, that I supported his belief that the world had badly treated him. And, stupidly as it turned out, the only answer I could come up with was to offer him a treat. Hoping that the gesture would be seen by him in a spirit of understanding of his troubles. So I'd said, 'Does tha like whelks?'

'Whelks??'

'Ahh,' I'd mumbled, going red and wishing I'd said a pint or a bag of humbugs or anything else for that matter. Because, to be honest, he couldn't have look more non-plussed if I'd pulled a coal shovel out and smacked him with it.

'Why?' Came his next one.

'Well . . . ah'll get thi' a plate if tha likes,' was all I could say, feeling dafter about it by the second.

'Ah've just swallowed a bacon and tomato sandwich,' he'd snapped, not hiding his disgust at this proposed mix.

'I know . . . ah were just trying to cheer thee up,' was all that I could think to say.

Not that it impressed him. Because, with no messing, he'd bluntly asked if I could stomach such things after a fry-up. And I had to be honest by admitting that I couldn't

'Well wot are tha pushing 'em onto me for then?' snapped his reply. And I'd groaned aloud, squirming in the knowledge that everyone else there was listening.

So, panic beginning to give way to anger at all this, I'd snapped back by explaining that it had been a poor attempt at cheering him up.

'Oh,' he'd said, heavy on the sarcasm now. 'Well . . . if tha wants to cheer me up buy us one o' dem,' and his hand had shot across me to point at a display of fresh custard tarts. Not, you'll notice, bothering with that rudiment of good manners known as saying 'please'.

I'd had it with him. Had it up to the teeth now after giving him a good half-hour of my time. Time he'd spent hammering me with hang-ups and hard luck stories which, by and large, I wasn't responsible for.

And whatever emotions towards him I had felt earlier now evaporated in my annoyance and rising ire. As far as I was concerned, having reached that point, Snuff was back to being what he'd always been as a little kid . . . a bastard pest.

So, deciding it was my turn to show it, I'd raised my voice. Demanding of the miserable sod serving that he be given the custard he preferred. And somehow, in all innocence, I detonated it all again. Because then it was her turn to start.

'Custard? He's just had a bacon and . . .' she began and went on about the effects it would have on his stomach. Shrill voiced, hands on thin hips and a look of disbelief when the chuff informed her of my original offer by way of a sweet. Loudly, cuttingly and sneeringly repeating the dreaded word of 'whelks'. Smirking at the pantomime we were performing.

So that I'd exploded at their treatment, banging down the two-bob piece to pay for it with a shaking hand.

'For Christ's sake give him one,' I'd grated. Staring hard into that snotty expression of her's. Adding with as much sarcasm as I could muster that, 'I'll eat his bleeding whelks for him'.

It was easy after that, knowing I had no more need of an excuse to leave. The market crowd would soon absorb me once I'd moved, glad to be breaking the contact, resolving to make this complaining midget one of the items from my past that was best forgotten. Filed away under the contemptuous heading of 'two penn'orth of copper'. That's all.

So I'd said, 'I'll sithee', relief driving out tension in that first step away.

But his hand, the one not holding the custard he was wolfing, reached out. Catching my sleeve and holding me. For a moment I'd laboured under the silly misapprehension that he regretted annoying me at the end. That he wanted to make amends for not making our meeting one of laughter and remembrance. That, whatever his complaints, his roots lay where mine did. And that those poor times as kids *had* been good, despite his wish to grow never being granted.

But no, his purpose was not of any of these. It had no connection with our past days. Rather was it a half-hearted query of, 'Are tha doing owt this Friday neet?' His eyes not on me but in the runny bits of yellow tart sticking to his fingers.

I'd struggled for careful words to answer him, not knowing why he should ask and scared of being trapped into another meeting with him.

'Only,' he'd gone on between licks, 'it's me stag neet . . . ah wondered of tha'd like a pint wi' me.'

And he left me stranded by it. Caught in a no-man's-land of wanting to be pleased for him without wanting any more of his company.

So I had lied without hesitation, claiming other commitments. Wishing him the best and offering my hand for him to shake. Immediately regretting it at the feel of the limp uselessness of the returned grip. Knowing from it that he'd no real desire to express pleasure in it.

I forced a smile and asked him to kiss the bride for me.

'Kiss her thissen,' he'd said. With no trace of concern at my obvious moves to leave quickly, he jerked a thumb at the spiteful-looking serving girlstood coldly watching us. 'That's her stood theer.'

Life, it struck me, had not yet finished playing cruel games with him.

Throwing out the Ash

LIFE DAWNED FOR ME in a tiny back-to-back house amongst the giant steelworks of Sheffield in September 1935, making me the seventh child of a brood which would eventually reach nine. As well as bathing me in the dubious rays of my grim birthplace.

It was a dirty place to begin. Dark and noisy from the big works surrounding it. One to make other better-placed areas look disdainfully down on, scornful of the hovering grey blanket from the outpourings of tall chimneys which permanently covered us, weaving a dirty mist which shut out the light in summer. So that gloom took away our sunny days.

Making those better off view our decorative plumes from their distant hills with shameful silence when visitors showed distaste for the vista sprawled beneath them in our valley. Neutrals who were unknowing of the sweated labour hidden from view, and caring little for its skill.

They judged us by sight, lightly dismissing any hurt caused by such ignorance as no more than local pride in the type of work being done, and snorting away our claim that world fame was worth the dirt, with the telling point that the price being paid for such material excellence was in our portrayed image.

Dirty Sheffield. Smoky Sheffield. A mucky place to live. Where I was born.

We were poor at my birth. Very poor, or so they tell me. Living cramped on the top of each other in a scabby little house in Attercliffe. One of the thousands covering the human element living huddled in amongst that cavernous mass of heavy plant. Our cross in life.

Living without most of the comforts we now know and harder than I would ever know, due to the longed-for work returning at a time to coincide with my arrival. Bringing with it the jobs and blessed wages long since forgotten in the terrible depression filling those

Chimneys beside the River Don, from Nursery Street, looking towards Lady's Bridge, probably in the 1920's.

desperately empty years of the 'twenties and 'thirties.

A never-ending time, they tell me, of enforced idleness when young men in their working prime – like my own father – could find nothing more productive to do save increase the size of their family.

An escape from reality which in today's money-obsessed society would be seen as socially irresponsible, yet one which then was a sign of a man's capability, wages or not.

This old-time fashion which ignored the physical barriers of living space and economics, intent on procreating sons and daughters. Right or wrong, it is one I am glad they followed, as in today's more comfortable climes I have the benefit of a numerous family, thrown up by a belief that didn't make sense and which the rich condemned. Until the war clouds gathered, and Prime Minister Baldwin failed in his attempts to appease Hitler, making Sheffield's idle hands the answer politicians and steel barons sought as the pace quickened towards the inevitable conflict of World War Two.

I cried a lot as a kid, so the elders say, and I unreservedly take their word for it. I have sisters who still remind me of the burden I was as they walked the midnight floor, cradling and patting and shushing me back into a sleep they themselves craved for.

'A mardy little sod . . . allus roaring,' as Violet the eldest put it, recalling my performances with that straight-to-the-point bluntness which always was her over-riding feature.

One that brooked no compromise as to whether hunger or colic might in some way have influenced those nightly protests. Whatever . . . it was her and the others who suffered it, and I have little option but to accept their version of my early encumbrance upon them. I just wish that she would be so readily honest about those times when my squawking must have driven them into inflicting painful reminders of how I was disturbing them. Not that I can prove it, my memory doesn't reach back that far. But the glint in her eye, and that of my late Mum, tell me that there were such nights, nights when I felt their hand.

Oh, what the hell, I'd asked for it and it hasn't lessened by one jot my affection for those who laid it on. So that, to this day, I am still unsure whether her cutting assesment of, 'Tha's not changed much, 'as tha,' when she tells me of those events is meant, or just another example of that dagger-thrust humour which played so big a part in our daily life then.

And I still remember the coldness striking deep at us in every part of the house, save for that small area around our coal fire. It was an icy thing, swamping our bedroom in its clammy cloak and bringing a dampness to the flock mattress we slept on, shivering together beneath grey ex-army blankets supplemented with coats not needed till the morning. Each of us scrabbling to lay claim with freezing feet to that heavy earthenware hot water bottle we took with us to bed. A mangle of jerking bare legs and searching toes that sought ownership of it in the beginning, and a total rejection when its smooth round body lost its comforting warmth in the night, and was kicked away in sleep as we dreaded the morning light, when the leaving of this collective warmth had to be faced yet again.

An ordeal to be hated. One where small reluctant feet were asked to meet that chilling grip the patterned oil-cloth covered floor waited to exert. Forming an unwelcome bond to our moist soles in our scurry to get downstairs, praying to be met by a smiling fire.

I loved that coal fire. We all did, no matter our age. Loved its glowing heat as another cold day began. Waiting for us at the living room door. Reaching out yellow-fringed flames to spread their height up the back of the iron range. Leaving glowing red embers within a barred grate that bore whispers of soot. Hanging as black pennants, remnants of a bygone fuel now burnt and dead and seen by us as pagan signs of things to come. A letter, a stranger, a birth or a death, money. All were foretold in those fluttering flags. Depending on how such things were read, and whether you believed its sign. Such was the way I remember.

One where central heating meant heat from a central point that went no further. One that we loved and missed when the fortnightly ration of four bags of coal exhausted itself yet again, leaving us without by a regularity that we hated. Causing us, and every family around, to wait in haste for the coalman. And, should his arrival fail, we would turn to any alternative in the way of wood, or old shoes and lino, or coke that had to be queued for at the gas works on Effingham Street. Anything that might breath life back into those dancing flames we loved. The ones that helped me on bitter mornings. When the house was cold . . . and oil cloth stuck to my feet.

Our's had a fireguard. A three-sided one, made to fit the entire length of hearth and oven. Metal framed with a mesh body to protect us from hot coals that might fall, without blocking their needed heat. Yet another friend. One that fathers parked perished bums on, and mothers gladly used as a dryer of clothes on wet washdays. One that kids like me were clipped around the ear for when caught pushing long tapers of paper through to set alight on the coals. Holding on as long as we dared, defying the flame inching its way along our tenuous grip. Watching in fascination the charred shreds breaking away to float down in bobbing circles, landing lightly in the dusty hearth or disappearing to nestle unseen behind the ashpan hiding the hot clinker and

waste. A silly game, and one that we took a chance in playing, risking scorched fingers rather than be the first to let go. One that oft-times ended with tears at being caught.

Strangely, that early aquaintance with fire proved to have a purpose. Because, at the age of nine, my father died and I nervously found myself to be the eldest male still at home, what with both elder brothers being away involved in the war. Which, in turn, meant that it now fell upon me to make that early morning fire I had enjoyed coming down to for so long. And I quickly learned it was one thing having the benefit of its welcoming smile to start the day, but quite another to be faced with the daunting task of actually lighting it.

I mean, there I'd be, shivering with a mixture of cold and a fear of failure. Standing before this dead and dirty friend of mine who seemed impervious to my forlorn dismay at finding him out.

But it had to be done, and lack of years and experience in such work could not be a reason for letting down those younger ones who depended on me. And knowing this, with the added incentive of my own coldness, brought home the effect of the old saying about the way in which the Lord helps those who help themselves.

I remember making many mistakes along the way of learning. Many times when it denied my efforts and pleas. Times when I'd be late for school from trying to give it life. Determined to be its master.

And slowly but surely I did improve. Did become more confident, more proficient. Until eventually I found myself no longer afraid of the task, more occupied with the speed I could now bring to generating its heat into our freezing living room. Bringing with its comfort a feeling of pride within at the grown-up skill I now had. One that placed me on a par with others much older who would normally view anyone of my size and age as 'nowt but a babby'. And I had felt pleased with what I'd done. Enjoying that feeling of not now being at the cold's mercy. I could now drive it out, make the place warm for the younger ones to come down to. Give to them that early blessing of heat which I had always loved in the times before, when I had come down to its welcome, never thinking of how it had got there. Or caring.

I discovered that its conception depended greatly upon my preparation for it. Of how the grate is its lungs, providing that life-giving draught of air to those elements of paper and stick which would give us lift-off.

And how neglect of that principle, by way of idleness in not clearing out the dead, usually rewarded me with a panic-filled frustration at the way it refused to light. Failure taught me better. It drove home the lesson of patience, of increasing the chance of success by following tried and tested ways.

So, I would carefully clear out that clogging ash still choking the grate from the night before. Cold fingers gripped a poker that I would rattle furiously between those layered bars. Driving out those useless lumps to fall impotently atop the small mountain of ash waiting for it in the recess below. A coloured mixture of solid white and grey dust. Lumpy by nature of its burnt life, finishing off as no more than twisted shapes of clinker. No use to man nor beast anymore. And only fit for hiding behind the ash pan covering it.

I hated the stuff for its dirtyness. And the way in which it formed a choking cloud that would swirl around me angrily as I shoveled it up into that old enamel bowl we kept for the job. Clumsily scraping at its pile with the special narrow-bodied tool which everyone had then.

Doing the best I could to see through eyes reduced to mere slits, and lips sealed in a battle to resist its attack upon my head and face.

And I still recall that enamel bowl's cumbersome weight as I'd rise unsteadily from my knees, holding out its bulk before me in the best way I could manage. Trying so hard not to spill any in a tottering walk to that rusty bin outside. Oft times pausing to lower it and rest, to renew an aching grip that made puny little arms complain. And twisting away my head as its stinging contents were caught up in the outside wind, sending up a bursting plume to shroud me yet again. As though to punish me for its disturbance, and the way in which it was having to make room for the new.

It was, without doubt, the one part of this ritual that I intensely disliked. Yet it had to be faced, otherwise that vital rush of air to the new fuel would be missing. That powerful thrust which I created by way of balancing a small shovel, edge first, on the top bar of the grate and stretching newspaper across it.

Believe me, the effect of it and the roar it made zooming up our chimney scared the life out of me to begin with. I would be knelt there, holding like hell to the edges of this newspaper to stop it being sucked away up the flue, hoping that those lumps of coal would light first time. Willing the twisted paper stumps I'd laid them on would prove an able substitute for the firewood we lacked. Igniting black nuggets, plucked from a bucket, filled and clumsily carried from a cellar reached by steep turning stone steps. Coal which smudged everything as you sorted it, judging those pieces best suited by size. To be carefully patterned over criss-crossed knotted strips of the Sunday Pictorial.

Yesterday's news took the place of those magic white firelighters you could buy in Curly Bradshaw's corner shop. If you had any money. Or things you could pawn.

I can close my eyes and still conjure up that scene of

Changing times

During the 1930's and '40's and right into the 1950's, Sheffield Council did a lot to replace sub-standard homes like those on Kent Road, Heeley, left, with a Town Hall vision of homes fit for heroes; these are on Herries Drive and were built just before the Second World War began in 1939.

It was to one of these improved homes, with inside lavatory, bath, electric light in all rooms and plenty of space and light that many Sheffield families were thankful to be moved before the Town Hall lost track of where and how its tenants wanted to live, and started building disasters such as Kelvin, Broomhall and Hyde Park.

me fearfully trying to encourage, whilst still control, that upward rush of air that lit our fire. Still feel that sense of alarm as those brown scorch marks began to appear on the face of that spreaded newspaper sheet across the shovel. Heralding the flames about to engulf and send the paper spiraling from my grasp as a terrifying torch to that soot-lined chimney breast.

A fire I did not need, and one that I desperately would try to snuff by screwing it into a burning ball before the draught could claim it and ignite the soot. Soot oin those days was a plague upon us that was hard to avoid, whether outside or in, by the way in which it fell from grey skies. Or caught alight in chimneys to spew out miniature comets as a firework display to delight the crowd who always gathered to watch such things. With kids who cheered each explosion of darting yellow-tipped flames forming patterns above in the cold sky. Erupting in burning showers from a chimney pot that acted as a cannon, making the crowd 'Ooo' and 'Aah' at each sizzling piece falling to earth before them.

Silly sods.

I remember those things. Remember them well, and the way I myself had felt the excitement of watching those volcanoes. With the clanging bells of fire engines rushing to help. Taking over this frightening event from the useless efforts of those inside who sought to douse the inferno falling within by placing bowls of water in the now dead grate. All thoughts of firelighting now defunct in the light of things gone wrong.

Choking, with smarting eyes they had fled. Seeking escape in the better air outside as they coughed away the acrid taste of it all. Looking into each other's stained faces with long stares of disbelief of how their eager desire for a fire could so quickly turn to this fear of it.

Not like now, of course. Not with all this modern stuff. You don't need, or see, the chimney sweeps we had to use then. When we had ten bob to pay for one that is. I remember standing behind him, one time when he cleaned ours.

He began by putting up this large green cover that stretched the whole length of our Yorkshire range. It had a hole in it, through which he inserted his rods one by one. Screwing the threaded end of the next one into the last end of the rod already up the chimney. Twisting these pliable shafts all the while to make that large bristled head being forced up the flue scour fiercely against the old brickwork. Dragging and driving the filthy clinging soot to fall in a series of whooshes. Avalanches of the stinking problem that collapsed from their hidden perch to make that green cover sag and bulge with their weight.

A cleansing that I watched as a kid, behind the sweep's kneeling figure. Marvelling as rod after rod was pushed into and through that great cloth hanging from our mantle piece, secured by several flat irons he'd brought with him.

Twisting and shoving and panting as he forced its path upwards, seeking that last push when the head would pop out of the pot. Spinning in triumph as a victory roll above our roof. Telling the world that we were clean once more in a banner wave. A big, lovely, and filthy black spinning wheel which we ran outside to see and cheer in excitement. Brought to us by courtesy of a soot-covered flat-capped character who arrived early morning with his rods and brushes over a shoulder.

Adding yet another page to the picture book of life that I can look back upon.

A blackened character who has gone, like so many others. Taking with him those shivering mornings of my past, to be thankfully and comfortably replaced by today's twenty-four hour round the clock finger-licking heat. Warmth that we don't measure by the number of lumps left to burn.

Laying to rest the ghost of Ben Kettleborough's coal lorry. That bottle-green painted relic of a flat backed ex-army Bedford work-horse which chugged and wheezed its way to us. Battling her way through those cruel winters, loudly protesting beneath those hundred-weight bags piled three deep on her back. Straining her springs and axle to the coaxing and cajoling cries of Ben and his two labourers crammed in her cab. Brawny arms reaching out through lowered windows to bang upon the dented door panels in rhythm to their shouts and demands. Urging her up those hard pulls in voices you heard above the squealing gears whining and grating from the load.

A welcome sight. One which we yearned for when the last vestiges of dusty 'slack' had been carefully scraped from the cellar's furthest corner. Three days before. Days which we faced with dread, and nights when going to bed early was the key to needed warmth. When we kept our socks on and dreamed of Ben coming whilst we slept, bringing us summat to burn in that old green lorry.

Another sight that I will never forget, whatever else may slip away. Always remember the poorness of it all, and the way in which the important things in life were lessons we learned so early. Running home from school to ask if he'd been. Hoping the answer would be 'yes'. Backed up by a roaring fire. And I recall envying this man, despite his uniform of muck and grime. Wishing hard that I could enjoy his status, his privilege. His universal popularity. And the joy of knowing that as him I'd never again know a cold morning.

Or the dread of reaching for that last lump of coal.

To be honest, he and his lads overawed us kids. And we'd stand there, mouths open, watching at the way they would place their backs to the lorry's edge. Strong arms reaching up and behind their cap-covered heads to grasp and grip the neck of the bag Ben had lifted and kneed into position for them.

And I would imagine myself having such strength as they'd stooped double beneath its bulk. Pulling it into the leather pad strapped to their back, grunting in those first steps forward. Black streaked faces peering up from beneath a filthy neb with eyes red-rimmed by contrast. Their free hand tucked behind supporting the weight to be carried.

Somehow, to my constant amazement, repeating this journey again and again and still having the strength to break into that jerking forward trot. Despite such posture, such incumbence, and the many long hours already done that day.

Men who looked upon this labour as a pennant declaring their manhood. A dirty flag to be held aloft for the rest of us to acknowledge. We weaker mortals who saw them as welcome Titans. Admirers who were more than willing to ignore the dirt they revelled in as a badge of trade. Grateful of their presence, and for what they bore us.

Again, men and work now gone. Lost in the progess we have seen, along with those heavy graded sacks we prized. Taking along words and names we grew with. Billy Burnett . . . Old King Cole . . . Nutty Slack . . . Best Bright . . . Ovals . . . Coalite . . . Anthracite. And that most contemptuous and inferior product of all called Shale. Bagged, weighed on heavy duty scales at the depot, and stacked. Ton upon ton upon complaining lorries, in tiers that lined their length and often made heavier by the driving rain.

Work done by strong arms and aching backs. Never once pausing to believe a day would dawn when their brute power would become obsolete, ending those longing waits we made standing before a window, watching and listening for the Bedford's groan. Beginning instead a time when a simple button or switch would do the work for them.

Snuffing out those inky black faces with yellow teeth glowing from them. Wiping everything clean in our cellars, without the need of going early to bed. Faded heroes now long gone but still fondly spoken of amongst we older ones.

Recalling them in many ways as, now and then, they reach out into the shadows of their past to bring them back. Telling their favourite stories, as I will when I tell of the day when snotty Pete Fairfax and me watched as Ben and his lads arrived in Salmon Pastures. Only to find they had a problem at Curly Bradshaw's place due to that miserable sod forgetting to unfasten his cellar grate.

For that was how coal came to us then. Down through the iron grate set outside the house and into the waiting cellar beneath. A grate we kept in place by hooking a chain through its grill to hang down the brick shute and fasten to a hook driven into a cellar wall. A rather crude and elementary means of security, I admit, but necessary in that it at least denied some drunken yob the means of chucking the grate through your window.

Anyway . . . Ben shows up this day full of goodwill to find Curly too busy robbing people in his shop to unfasten the grate. Leaving the coalman tapping his steel-capped boots on the cobbles in strained impatience . . . don't you know. And not being any more enamoured of Curly than the rest of us, he resolved all of this annoying business by telling his lads to dump the four bag allowance right there on the shop front. Then, making the telling point of 'let's see if he can use a shovel better than his bacon slicer' he'd ordered his lads back aboard his old waggon and was gone.

Well, me and Pete had watched all of this open mouthed, outside of Curly's unimpressive emporium. Rather nonplussed at the new frontage which was now in everyone's way. With Curly inside, no doubt secretly pressing on the scales to rob some poor bugger out of a full ounce. Totally unaware of the temptation presented to me outside to relieve him of some coal to supplement our own measly three bags, that being all that my widowed Mum could afford at the time.

Pete's his panic of the consequences should we be caught in any way put me off. Not that I made a habit of taking other people's stuff. Far from it. Believe me, in those days kids were in no way protected from deserved punishment by the out-of-hand liberalism we're lumbered with now. Ask any lad of my age about his Dad's belt and you'll get confirmation of that.

It was just that, on this occasion anyway, I didn't feel that pinching a bit of Curly's coal ration was in any way worse than him pinching our rations in the way of food. A common practice, which he lost little sleep over. And one nosy Rosy Crapper made clear about the day she queued up for a bit of balm to make her weekly bread-cakes.

Curly, unaware that she was in, was in the process of totting up some prices he'd written on a pile of grease-proof paper sheets he wrapped our stuff up in. Gripping that stub of a pencil that he always dabbed on his tongue as he went about the task he enjoyed most . . . telling you how much to pay.

Anyway, he's in the middle of all this when the dulcet tones of our street's own town crier came floating over to warn Curly's current victim about watching him closely seeing as how he'd 'trained that bleeding pencil to add up wrong', an interjection which I can assure you was not appreciated, from a source Curly always described as a 'gobby cow'.

'Ah aluus know when tha'r in,' he'd snarl at her, 'cos it's only time we get a swarm o' flies in here'.

'Aah,' she would yell back over the scarf-covered heads of the others in front, 'and they'll need a pair o' bleeding glasses to land on owt wot tha's cut, an' all'. A stringent riposte that brought a glazed look to angry eyes already bulging in his flushed face.

But enough of his charisma, and back to the day I attempted to top up our coal ration with his by rejecting any thoughts of guilt for the reasons mentioned, as well as snotty Pete's paranoia over getting caught and not sharing my sense of adventure in robbing the swine.

But then again, his need at home wasn't as great as ours. He was lucky enough to have a Dad alive and working, which meant that they could afford their full ration. In fact he told me that what with his Mam at work all day and him at school they didn't light their fire till tea-time. They even managed to have some left when the next delivery came. This was unheard of at our house, we were always trying to scrounge a bit. So you see it all added up to him not really feeling my need. Which gave me a problem in my intent to rifle Curly's wayward coal.

So I decided to change tack with him. To exploit a known weakness he had with outright bribery. Bartering for his aid by offering to approach Mary Whetton, a lass in our class that he positively drooled over, yet dare not speak to. Not that he had a cat in hell's chance of getting anywhere, mind you. Not with her Mam bringing and fetching her back from school each day, watching over her like the proverbial hawk, so to speak. Giving any lad who so much as dared to smile at her lass a look that would have stopped a clock.

But . . . that was his problem. Mine lay there on this shop front. Looking far more attractive, to me anyway, than half-a-dozen Mary Whettons. Especially as she never seemed to talk about owt else except what it was like when she'd had her tonsils out.

Anyway, I'd shot off home to grab this old sack which I used to cover the wire netting front of my rabbit hutch at night, before returning post-haste should Curly get wind of the imminent peril befalling his next week's fire.

Back on site, with me pressing hard against the corner wall, nervously peeking out to see if my prey was still at bay, adrenalin pumping away through me like a trip hammer at the sight of it as I'd hoarsely whispered instructions for Pete to follow me in a crouching run. To position himself atop the coal pile unseen, and to monitor any movement of the unloved grocer inside his shop as I frantically stuffed his lumps into the sack.

And it worked, despite the terrible trembling of my legs as those sharp pieces hurt the fingers I used to grab and hide each piece that I pinched. Letting greed spoil the success of it by exceeding what meagre strength remained in that sack's ancient webbing. So that as the pair of us made our escaping dash on legs that wobbled from the weight strung between us it breathed its last. Ripping and spewing forth around our feet the prize I had so daringly gained. Stirring afresh all the fear already suffered once on the pile of coal, to drive us on a stumbling flight of escape. Ankles bending painfully on those uneven lumps as we sought to stay upright and still clutch the sack between us.

Until, inevitabley, our balance was lost. And Pete fell heavily. Splitting open the chin of his gasping mouth as it crashed against the unforgiving hardness of a doorstep, making him scream with shock and pain of it all, killing off the remaining strength I had at the sight of his blood. The crimson streaks of it showed between fingers he clutched the wound with. So that I'd begged and urged him back to his feet, convinced that his wails would stir Curly to come out and discover what I had attempted to take from him. Knowing full well the level of retribution to follow on from his unforgiving nature. And not wanting to meet it.

So I had fled. Having failed. Fled in panic, gripping and pulling on the snot-covered sleeve that Pete pressed to his bleeding chin. Making him run from the evidence laid around us on the stones with rotten sacking intermingled in its pattern.

Thinking only to get away, of how I'd be for it should Pete allow the sight of his blood to induce him into revealing my conspiracy to his Mam when she demanded reasons for it. And of how those lovely lumps would have burned for us had fortune been kinder to me that day.

Now I don't suppose that Pete, should he ever read this, will look back on that day with a large degree of fondness. Or share the smile it raises in me at the mental picture of the pair of us running like ruptured ducks with that sack of coal slung between us. No doubt he would scowl and point to the scar under his chin where they stitched it and blame me for it. But, that aside, it does hopefully give you some idea of the value which we placed then upon the black stuff. Along with the esteem we placed upon the likes of Ben and the lengths we'd go to in getting hold of his wares.

But, as I said, we don't see his like anymore. Just as today's kids don't have to look out for the dreaded School Board man as we did.

Now he was the bloke who came knocking when you lost a lot of time from school, whether it be from sickness or 'wagging it'. And the mere sight of him in his long belted raincoat and trilby hat coming up your street with that register under his arm checking door numbers, literally sent kids and their Mams diving upstairs into bed. The idea of that being that should he refuse to go away you could plead illness for the long

delay in answering him see. Talk about power? Arthur Scargill would have voted Tory for it. For that feller would petrify a solid street in seconds just by walking down it for fun.

Mind you, schooling was taken very seriously by the family then. And to be off meant that you daren't be seen in the street. Well, not until after school hours, anyway. You soon got pulled if you tried, believe me. There'd always be someone giving you a nasty look and saying something. Neighbours or shopkeepers or anybody passing would stop and question your presence.

'Shunt thaa be in school, lad?'

'No.'

'Why not?'

'Ahm badly . . . ah keep going short o' breath.'

'Short o' breath?' . . . thi mother'll be short o' bleeding breath if school board man sees thi.'

And it wasn't unknown for them to report you, either. Be it from spite or a genuine belief of acting in good faith towards your future. And then, on his arrival, the excuses would start. Lies and blatant untruths which you could tell from his stony expression he didn't believe one syllable of.

You'd had the mumps, whooping cough, diarrhoea, ear-ache, bad throat, lost your voice, fell down some steps, fell up some steps, burnt your hand making the fire, your shoes had no soles, your Mam was sick and you'd had to go to the pawn shop in her place, etc.

Owt, in fact, that would reasonably explain away those missing ticks in his book, those days he demanded account for. Glorying in the air of authority he exuded, and the nervousness he brought to kids and grown-ups alike. And I still recall the exaggerated emphasis of that book snapping shut at the end of his ominous lecture of how me and my Mam would be hauled before a panel in Leopold Street Education Offices if things didn't

Chucky Morris

CHUCKY WAS A SPIV. At least, that's what everybody called him and his sort during, and just after, the last war. And if you're not familiar with that term, then don't ask me why we called them that. Because I don't know. I just remember getting up one morning and learning a new word.

Just like when I'd got up on another day to discover that we'd suddenly invented this new and ridiculous cartoon figure called Kilroy. A drawing for us to laugh at with his hairless head and this morose expression on a face half covered by a brick wall that he peered over. His long nose acted as a pointer to the catch-phrase chalked beneath him, stating that 'Kilroy was Here'. Giving us something to chuckle over without really knowing why. Triggering off this national mania to reproduce his effigy on every conceivable place that chalk or paint could adhere to. On walls and doors and railway bridges, on steamy windows of shops and trams and trains. On tin roofs and the insides of school desks. In the grimy muck caking a furnace door and even looking down on you from the tiled urinal as you sought relief.

Kilroy, that ubiquitous, silent and ridiculous lifter of spirits we all loved, finding something encouraging in the way his gloomy presence dispersed the weight of dark and austere days. Kilroy made us laugh when laughter was at a premium. And every little helped.

Devastation in wartime central Sheffield, just after the 1940 bombing. The tram is climbing Angel Street.

Unlike Chucky, the hated wide-boy and black-marketeer. The sort who openly scorned others endlessly queuing on bitter cold and wet days, the young alongside the patient old, clutching tightly at wickerwork baskets or leatherette shopping bags that rested wetly against shivering legs, or hung, empty and flat, from icy wrists poking out from inadequate pockets which did their best to protect frozen fingers too cold to grip handles anymore. Perhaps a woollen headscarf, often fashioned turban-style in those times, doing what it could to deflect searching winter winds from painful ears as feet stamped the pavement, urging circulation back into limbs that had long since given up on warmth.

That is how they would stand. Patiently prepared to take their turn, swapping banter, rumour and tit-bits of scandal in their efforts to defeat the time it was taking, and the discomfort felt. Ration books closely guarded with a zeal which signified the importance of these coloured passports to whatever might be on offer that day, providing, of course, that whatever it was held out long enough for them to reach the front of the queue.

And finally having reached that point the overwhelming sense of injustice, even loud disgust, that such patience and orderliness should be rewarded by the paltry amounts which the coupons allowed, tiny shares of food which stern-faced shopkeepers carefully weighed and measured. Portions amounting to an ounce or less at times, making the space left in their bag highlight the ridiculous optimism in bringing such a large one along. All the same, it never stopped them from bringing it. Just in case. And to return home with something in it, no matter how small, was always better than queuing for nowt.

Yet somehow they fed us, doing it by a combination of minuscule allowances and the application of that old adage that 'necessity is the mother of invention'.

Day after day. Creating by their own imagination, and the information adverts from the Ministry of Food which were always shown just before the big picture at the cinema, a variety of tasty additions to help fill hungry bellies. Eking out such items as just over two pounds weight of meat, two ounces of corned beef, one pound of bacon, twelve ounces of cheese and the four fresh eggs which a family of four was expected to consume in a week.

We were allowed half-a-pound of butter, a pound of margarine, half-a-pound of tea and two pounds of sugar. Six pints of milk, a tin of dried milk and another of egg powder. There'd also be half-a-pound of lard, a pound jar of jam and, for us kids, the mind-blowing treat of twelve whole ounces of sweets to be shared.

A box of cornflakes used up four of the five weekly points, as did two pounds of rice pudding or unsweetened biscuits. Rare commodities such as pork sausage, fresh cod, liver, oranges and apples and onions only came from either hours stood in the afore-mentioned queues, or by way of an understanding with the appropriate shop. Or, to get back to the main purpose of all of this . . . the spiv.

Hopefully, that will give the reader some idea of the size of the problem women faced in feeding us in the 1940s. But they did it. And they did it by taking those amounts which today you would probably waste, building them up with items which were plentiful, such as bread and potatoes and carrots and swedes and turnip and cabbage and parsnip and tomatoes. So that no-one ever faced a full day on an empty plate. I know we didn't.

To this day I still remember how turnip mixed with potato doubles its own quantity. How rabbits were queued for at six o'clock in a morning before the fish market even opened, because of the delicious stew they made. A smell which even now, a lifetime on, brings back mental pictures of me standing sniffing at our back door after running home from school on cold days.

And I mind how the greasy gravy of it was carefully stored on a cold pantry shelf for the following day, to be re-heated and devoured with thick crusty bread. There was boiled tripe with onion, if you got lucky. Chicklings and Bag. Oat cakes and pikelets and home-grown rhubarb stalks which I craftily dipped into the precious sugar basin if no-one was looking. Caraway seed cake and greengage jam which came in tins and never tasted better than when smeared onto thick toast made by the heat of a glowing coal fire. And would you believe – horse and whale meat?

I never had either myself, but I clearly recall queues outside a shop on Spital Hill with these dubious substitutes for a good old-fashioned roast-beef joint. Still, the thought that these bloody lumps displayed on trays might have been pulling your milk float last week didn't stop people from buying and cooking it, despite putting up with wisecracks such as 'I hope that's the sodding thing I backed at Kempton Park'. As I said . . . nowt was wasted. Not even sympathy.

Which is why gardens were turned over to the production of every vegetable you could get to grow. Even front gardens. People took to keeping hens and ducks to enjoy the luxury of regular eggs, as well as solving many a Christmas dinner problem for them or any neighbour in a position to return the favour with yet another missing treat. So that, by and large, all of these things, and others which time has erased, played their own significant part in those days of little choice. Doing their bit for the war effort. Helping to keep back the enemy of hunger which we kids dreaded. Forever hoping that there would be 'summat for us tea'.

None of which, of course, bothered Chucky and his ilk. For he lived in a well protected sphere that was free from the annoyance of shortage which a long war inflicted upon the rest of us. No . . . in his case, just like in the cowboy films we watched, the waggon train always got through.

His was a world where a whispered word or a nod and a wink took away the long cold queue. Where a simple point in the right direction led un-erringly to a land mystical, where all was plenty, made up of a cornucopia of the things others desired yet couldn't have. A secret place known only to those who knew someone . . . who knew someone who knew. An under-the-counter industry where beef and pork and lamb and alcohol and fags and chocolate and silk stockings and clothing coupons and petrol hung on trees. All the ordinary things which turn longing into the comfort of reality, things that today we rightly take for granted.

All of these and many more were hanging there in that kingdom of plenty, waiting to be plucked, making a cruel mockery of our general and näive belief that everyone was 'doing their bit'. Labouring under that admirable misconception that being British meant that no-one cheated. We learned that a crafty word into a crafty ear along with sufficient capital to hand eliminated any need to day-dream on frozen feet. It made possible those mundane things which in my childhood assumed an importance which today's youth would laugh at. Courtesy of Chucky . . . the spiv.

Now, strangely enough, despite the anger of those going without, the daftness in all of this lay in the duplicity of attitudes shown towards him. For on the one hand he could be reviled as little more than a criminal parasite, feeding on the weakness of human nature. Yet on the other he could be actively sought out, sucked up to, should the possibility present itself of some longed-for goody dropping into your basket.

Silencing with it all the previous and vociferous

hostility at a stroke as it soothed the hurt of being left out. 'It's all wrong,' they would say. Unless, that is, you were getting some. And then you didn't cry so loud. Didn't condemn so quick all those butchers and bakers and Jack-the-lads who could make such things happen. For all that you needed to do was to accept a system which made all things possible . . . at a price.

So how, you might ask, did you get in on this intricate network where the right word opened those doors leading to material privilege? And had you been there to ask at that time, then in most cases the answer would have been the same. We didn't know. And the reason we didn't know was simply because we never had enough money to find out. Perhaps if we had, then I wouldn't be writing about the corruptness of it all.

In fact, had the financial climate of our family then been more healthy, no doubt I would now be recording how we'd spent those war years being eternally grateful to Chucky. God-blessing him from the gratitude I'd felt from being rescued from the surfeit of 'taters and beetroot which went towards making our staple diet. But, all things being equal, we didn't have the coin to afford his kind. Which in turn meant that we got nowt from him. And that being so, while-ever I'm telling the story anyway, that made him in our view nowt else but a scum bag. But . . . that's life.

Or, as Chucky would have said . . . that's war. And long may it prosper.

Men like Chucky were nothing more than grey phantoms to kids my age. And, not surprisingly, seeing as we were all getting a first-hand experience of this harsh rationing in force, our childish opinions of his kind had to be coloured by the outrage shown by our betters. An indoctrination of our feelings which meant woe betide any lad or lass walking into our school yard sucking a toffee twice in the same week. Because such

an obvious declaration of unfairness to the rest of us would have resulted in their back being thumped that many times they'd have either swallowed it too soon or spat it out. Either way they wouldn't have got to enjoy it. Not without us getting a lick.

As a classic example of this determination to make others share their good fortune let me recall for you the time when my mate Harry Owen followed Betty Clithero all over school trying to get his hand inside this paper bag she'd brought, which held a few pieces of mint rock her mother had somehow obtained.

Now Betty hated him. Always had done from the day when he'd helped Tommy Jessop shove a live newt down her jumper neck. So Harry, despite his grabs and manoevring stood no chance of getting her to share. Anyway, to get his own back for this failure, he'd waited until she'd gone for needlework with all the other lasses and then pissed into her inkwell.

And what she couldn't understand afterwards was why her writing in the exercise book was a lighter blue than ours. Plus the added problem of her blotter not being able to dry her work without obliterating half of the words. Harry, as you might well imagine, felt suitably avenged.

Not that it was any different with the grown-ups. For should any feller flash a packet of Senior Service or Players or Capstan Full-Strength cigarettes in a pub, he'd cause a shock wave of silence quicker than the ale running out. And Lord help a woman who walked in wearing proper stockings instead of the universal leg paint.

Because, without a doubt some 'lady' would make sure that she left carrying more ladders in them that the AFS used. So you see, that well-used fallacy about the way everyone mucked in together during the last war was a bit of a 'porky' really.

Well, it was on the home front, as I've tried to illustrate with these examples. And the influence of rubbish like our friend-in-need, Chucky, a man around whom stories abounded, embellished through repeated tellings until they couldn't possibly bear resemblance to the true event. As it always is, and always will be, with those whose way of life takes them outside the herd. Which is something that I'm glad of, really, because had he been a run-of-the-mill miserable soul I wouldn't have this tale to tell.

Now, or so it goes, Chucky had that intrinsic something that draws you towards people who are different by choice. To some he was a hero for the things he could get them, to others a low life for doing it. He was a clever sod for the way in which he constantly broke the rules which others feared. Or he was brainless for risking the punishment that went with being caught. He was a coward for brazenly cheating his way out of joining the armed forces. Or, to those he helped, he was doing more good staying at home. And so on.

As I said earlier, it all depended on whether you could afford him. As Ria Thorpe, her down our way with the rampant spit, commented with chattering teeth one freezing day to old Mrs Flynn as they patiently queued outside Bostock's the butchers on Attercliffe Common following a reliable rumour that he'd got some kidneys in that he didn't want others to know about, 'Ah don't give a cow what anybody calls him, if he brings a nice piece of brisket wi' him he can put his feet under our table any time he likes'. Poor old Mrs Flynn, doing her best to dry her splattered face with the end of her scarf, could only grate her false teeth and snap back that Chucky would be better off leaving the brisket and bringing a 'chuffing Turkish towel wi' him instead'. Ria had refused to be drawn.

Anyway, back to this Chucky character who lived somewhere up Grimesthorpe Road in Pitsmoor, occupying a house very much in the style of ours except for the cellar. For whereas ours was full of damp, his was full of all the goodies that honest corner shops could only dream about.

Now that I mention it, damp was one of the few things in good supply then. In fact you could have as much as you liked. It was there when you got into bed, and it was waiting for you next morning when you got dressed again. All without a ration book and all.

Anyway, Chucky's place was piled high with the sort of things that had nosey Rosy Crapper gob-smacked when she'd burst un-announced into Edna Duffy's tiny kitchen to relay gossip just obtained whilst pawning her best shoes.

'You've never seen so much,' she gurgled, ignoring the venomous glare of Edna's husband, Sam, sat studying the horses in his *Daily Herald*. A man not blessed with neighbourly love towards this woman he once described as that 'bleeding pest in a turban'. In fact, on one occasion he got so mad at his wife for keeping her talking that he'd stormed into the front room, seized the poker and vented his anger by furiously ramming it in and out of the fire grate.

This caused a red-hot coke to shoot out onto the peg rug and him to dash back into the kitchen for some water, only to trip over Rosy's big foot and fall face first into the washing mangle, breaking a tooth in the process. Which just shows that Chucky didn't have sole rights to the privilege of upsetting the whole populace. Anyway, back to this spiv.

Now, apparently, there was at least one thing about Chucky that everyone seemed to agree on. He was no lover of anything remotely connected to the military. Although one story said that it didn't put him off sheltering this Yank one time who'd gone AWOL up here. He was supposed to have charged the poor sod twenty-five quid to let him hole up for a couple of nights in that famous cellar. Nobody ever proved it but, twenty-five quid? Jesus, for that kind of loot he could have slept in the Grand Hotel on Leopold Street. And had an egg for his breakfast.

Naturally he'd laughed off the rumour, preferring instead to repeatedly insist that his willingness to serve King and Country had been overruled at his call-up medical when it was discovered that he had an 'irregular heartbeat', a reason which didn't go down well at all amongst his critics. As Billy Whittaker, the landlord, told a crowded bar in the *Dog and Duck* one night, 'There's more frigging chance of F-F-F-Freddie Thorpe reading the Home Service news than him having a bad heart'. A comparison that Chucky didn't like apparently, because as a consequence of that assessment Billy found himself crossed off the Christmas list when Chucky shared out the ciggies to other hostelries in our area. Proving the point that truth has to be paid for.

All the same, despite his tricks, the spiv couldn't escape public service altogether. Not many did. And in his case they roped him into the Home Guard, despite his indignant protests viz-a-viz his suspect heart condition.

But, manpower being at a premium, he had it to do. And like it or not found himself out at night in lousy weather guarding of all places High Hazels park against the off-chance that a German paratrooper might call in. Or crawling on his wet belly through filthy allotments around Darnall practising how to garotte with a piano wire such an unwanted guest, should one ever turn up. They even ran to giving him two live rounds to fire just in case things should ever reach that critical stage. A gesture he would no doubt have found comical seeing as how with his connections he could have kitted his platoon out with enough of the stuff to start another Russian Front.

But, to their loss, they never appreciated his talents, eventually having words with him after being caught practicing his new-found strangling skills on some poor bugger's flock of ducks on a patch which his section had been detailed to guard.

'He must have had a shipping order in,' Billy Whittaker had snarled upon being informed by nosy Rosy, no doubt still smarting over his exclusion from the last festive ciggy dividend as he'd banged down before her the usual bottle of Jubilee Stout.

Then, grimacing at having to fish out the coppers she'd deliberately placed in one of the numerous beer puddles on his bar, he'd added, 'It's a pity one o' dem ducks weren't a German bomb in disguise'.

Rosy had turned away, grinning at how her gossip had upset him. Muttering on her way back to her table that should Chucky ever attempt to perform such a summary execution upon this snivelling landlord he'd need a 'bleeding bullrope to choke thee, yer tight sod'.

Still, leaving that aside, Chucky soldiered on, hating this disruption to his commercial interests, what with working during the day as a slinger at Brown Bailey's and then rolling about on wet grass most of the night.

So, having put up with this for about two months, he went and had an earnest chat with old Dr Hudson. He emerged waving medical evidence that all of this barmy nocturnal nonsense looking out for Germans who never showed up was most undoubtedly doing his dicky heart no good at all. Which I've no doubt was a massive relief to him and, I'll bet, an impressive benefit to old Hudson's liquor cabinet. And it must have been worth every bottle because, having slipped that particular noose, he then proceeded to avoid the ARP and Fire Warden duty, blithely waving the magical note at whatever organisation called him to account.

'This,' he would laugh as he tapped on the supposed dicky ticker, 'is what's known in medical circles as a Victor Sylvester,' gloating into the puzzled faces of those drinking alongside him. 'Yer know, slow, slow, quick-quick, slow.' And his cronies would bray loud and long as yet another crisp white fiver sprang from his bulging wallet to pay for yet another round.

Such was his way, his style. Posturing at a bar. Smug in knowing that he was the pinion which turned the wheels, which lifted the doors, behind which lay all those things which we now walk past in boredom. Never the less, the spiv was a fact of our young life. And sometimes a painful one at that, as Sam Duffy, who shared our street, found to his cost on the one and only occasion that he pitched his cap against this strutting parasite.

Now Sam, should you be unaware of his presence in my earlier books, was blessed with the gift of being able to amuse others without knowing he was doing it. Not deliberately, mind you. Things just happened to him.

So let's begin on the day Sam Duffy came home from work to be greeted by Edna breaking the news of his impending fatherhood, an event that in time turned out to be a daughter and the only child they would be blessed with. Something that Edna always saw as a sad loss, but one that he'd always dismissed with the callous remark that there wouldn't have been anymore anyway, 'now that ah know what's causing it'.

Anyway, there he is this particular night in question doing rough justice to a big Yorkshire pudding in onion gravy when she casually drops it out that at long last he's managed to do something right. Before propelling herself forward to snatch up his pot of tea and clumsily bang it against his teeth to try and wash down the lump that he's choking on.

So, as you might guess, it was not what you would call the ideal way of being informed of such glad tidings. But, gut instinct warned him that whatever it was that had begun for him then, sooner or later along the way something would go wrong. And he was right, of course.

It was a selfish attitude, being more sure of a problem cropping up than worrying over the long and trying pregnancy faced by his wife. But then he was no different to any other man I remember. Having done his bit in this oft-repeated ritual, he kept out of it. Better now, as the system demanded, leave her to the closeness of other females. Seeking the safety of his pub rather than enduring those frequent mood swings and bizarre cravings which beset her in those early weeks of pregnancy.

Behaviour that not only baffled him, but also scared him by making him lose control of this woman he thought he knew. Not knowing what to expect from her on coming back from work or full of ale. And not liking one bit his own relegation to a secondary role behind the consuming force of her whims and fancies.

Until the night when her restlessness in bed went on so long into the early hours that his longing for sleep drove him to angrily demand to know its cause. Tearfully and wistfully she had told him of the incessant pressure she was struggling with to suppress this unfathomable desire to taste once again the delicious experience of a childhood treat, stirred from its dormancy by the condition he had placed her in. Making him soften towards her, for once showing a recognition of the forces she was being tormented by. Asking her to let him share the burden of it, telling of his willingness to try all ways to provide that which racked her and spoiled his sleep. Making her cry in relief and love for his concern as she'd poured out her desperately felt need.

'A coconut?' He'd shot up in bed and yelled, convinced that he'd misheard her, that the twitching of her hidden body was from laughter at the joke she'd made and not from more crying.

'Wheer?' He'd pleaded to her blanket-covered head. 'Wheer do ah get thee one? Ah'm not Tarzan's bleeding monkey, tha knows, go on, tell us, wheer do ah get hold of one?'

And he'd banged his clenched hands against the mattress, making her whimpering form bounce with the impact. Leaving a tense silence to pervade them, which eventually broke with faltering words in which she'd explained how as a child her father had won one at a fairground he'd taken her to at Owlerton.

How the sweet richness of its milk drunk through the hole he'd punched, and the fibre of its inners had made it one of those childhood treats never forgotten. How she now craved its repeat and how she could think of nothing but that long hidden taste, brought back to life by his baby.

It had touched him, burying the fear and alarm he had felt at first with an understanding. Yet having to point out to her in a gentle manner that he knew of no way by which he could ease this problem.

'Yer cud ask him,' she'd sniffed. Encouraged by his softening.

'Who?'

She hadn't replied at first. Timing her reply for when his breathing was more even. Knowing her answer would cause him to panic.

'He cud get us one, him they all talk abaht, that spiv.'

Sam had lifted up to rest on his forearm. Looking hard at her half-covered head laid beside him.

'Chucky Morris?'

The name, never mind the thought of seeking him out, filled our lad with a complex mix of fear and excitement.

'But ah don't know him.'

'Rosy does,' she'd said, pulling the cover from her hidden face to look at him. Sensing that he might be weakening to her. Not aware of his real thoughts.

'Oh, she would, wunt she,' he'd snapped, aggressiveness returning at this unforeseen obstacle. 'That bleeding thing knows more than t'BBC.'

'Ike Mosely,' she jumped in. 'She told me that you have to see him first. He goes in the *Staniforth Arms* every night'.

She paused at that, letting him have time to absorb, to clear his thoughts of nosy Rosy. Waiting for a sign, a positive sign, that he'd do it.

'Will yer?' she asked again. Softly. Turning towards him, letting a comforting hand slide over his ample belly to give his waist an encouraging squeeze.

'Yer could do it,' she encouraged. 'He'll help yer, it dunt matter if he sez no, just try will yer? For me?'

And he'd turned on his side towards her, pressing up to gently kiss the top of her head.

'Bloody coconut. Never heard owt like it. Wunt tha like a new pinny instead?'

And so it began. This saga of wartime cunning in which our lad Sam set out to be a hero. Twice. Once for his missus, and the other for the glory of waving his success under the nose of Billy Whittaker and all of those who saw him as a figure of fun. Which would have made a smashing ending to all of this. But, and if you've read my stuff about him before then you'll have guessed, things never seemed to follow the simple course he plotted. So that, once again, not appreciating that success in his dream depended entirely on a correct method of approach in the twilight world he was about to enter, this barm pot went barging in.

Blithely thinking along the lines that you first found

the elusive Chucky, then told him what you wanted, and he wrapped it up nicely with pink ribbon. Unfortunately it wasn't like that. There was chain to follow. A complicated ritual designed to protect those along its length from not getting their 'cut'. And seeing as our lad had a natural aversion towards paying anything at the best of times, you will recognise that such a careful approach towards spending loaded the dice somewhat heavily against him in this rather one-sided game. To him the exercise was simple. Find this spiv, buy him a pint, tuck the prize under his mac, then sod off back to Attercliffe where the ale would no doubt be cheaper. Alas, as with all manner of things connected with this natural conductor of disaster, it all went wrong. Again.

It had begun well with him tracking Ike Mosely in the pub mentioned. Now Ike, who rode the streets on a converted Raleigh bike he'd rigged up to drive a grinding wheel to sharpen knives and scissors, was the first link in the greasy chain. You wouldn't have thought so to look at him, but then, you wouldn't have wanted by choice to look at him anyway. He had the kind of squinty features only a River Don rat would have taken a shine to.

Anyway, Ike's sat there in a corner playing crib, the first two fingers of his right hand burnt deep brown by the nicotine effect of countless Woodbines. Proof positive to Sammy boy that clearly here was someone who knew someone. Evidence to make his breathing quicken with conviction that here was his man. So that he threw caution to the wind by marching straight over. Casting aside even an introductory gambit of 'How do,' to demand loudly of the said creep, 'Do they call thee Ike? Are tha a pal of Chucky Morris?'

Now, were you the more polite sort, you would say that he'd chosen his opening words badly. On the other hand and lacking such benefit my sort would have

Looking down Waingate towards Norfolk Market Hall in the 1950's.

described such a shit-brained approach as 'mekking a reight bollocks of it'.

Whatever, Ike's silent response was a cold-eyed perusal of our dumpling's figure, finishing it off with an icy stare into the lad's well-flushed face. Something that he wouldn't have dwelt on so long had he been aware that his opponent used this diversion to slyly cheat by moving Ike's marker peg back down the crib board, thereby lessening the margin he was losing by. This little observation on my part has nowt to do with this story, but does illuminate the type of people Sam was dealing with.

Anyway, back to basics. With Ike questioning Sam's knowledge of his secret whereabouts and him revealing nosy Rosy Crapper's extensive range of information, he'd sat himself down on a spare stool at the table. Ike had tossed his head back at the name, recognising her fame. Pushing his now empty glass Sam's way, with the cold-voiced enquiry of 'has tha tried t'ale in here?'

Now at this point in the tale I'd like you to note that

Ike's misplaced anticipation of a positive response to this obvious request for a bribe showed an appalling lack of knowing just who he was dealing with. For had he but known it he was now in direct opposition to the lad's one strength. Namely that getting Sam to buy you a drink was on a par to getting took home in the royal carriage. Which explains Sam's bewilderment at the winks and nods coming his way, and Ike's growing annoyance at no sign of movement. Until, for Ike anyway, the penny dropped that here was someone lumbered with that pre-war innocence that Ike would be glad to oblige for nowt. Or, he was now faced with the type commonly referred to in his circles as having 'short arms and deep pockets'.

Either way, he didn't like what he saw.

'Has tha ever done owt like this afore?' Ike asked, coming straight to the point.

Sam had shook his head. Explaining that it was Edna's pregnancy that was the root cause of his odyssey.

'She's going mad for a coconut,' he'd said, straight faced.

Ike had listened, bent forward, and equally serious about it had ridiculed his reason by asking, 'Wunt she rather 'ave a little girl instead?' Again he lifted his empty glass to place it firmly in front of Sam

'Fill it,' he'd snapped, not prepared to tolerate any more näivety or meanness. 'And while tha's at it get her a Guinness'. He nodded at a dreadful looking woman sat opposite, with a mass of greasy black hair stuffed inside a hairnet big enough for a Grimsby trawler.

Now Sam, alarmed at the growing cost which these ugly people were heaping on him, felt moved to complain that he hadn't come to 'throw a bleeding party, tha knows'. And Ike had reacted to this complaint by pointing to a sparrow-like older woman wearing a man's scarf over her head, chewing God-knows-what in a toothless mouth, who'd just come in and who was making her way toward the greasy black-haired one by saying, 'and that's her mother. She likes a pint of mixed'.

The tram ride back to town seemed to Sam afterwards to take ages. For this was definitely not how he had envisaged things to happen. And the thought of going into Sheffield at night filled him with a dread of what lay ahead. It was a dark and unfamiliar place busy with strangers who passed as shadows without speaking. Bumping him without even a cursory 'Sorry, old luv,' as they would have done outside of Banner's.

Shivering and vulnerable, he'd made his way to stand in the doorway of the *Gaiety Vaults* where Ike, having extracted his toll, had said Sam must go. And he'd cursed the knife grinder for it, not reckoning on finding himself placed in such hostile environs. Fueling a sense of grievance already inflamed by the cost of those inveigled drinks and the tram fare. And the way in which Edna had exploited her condition to get him into all of this, forcing him out of the cocoon of safety Salmon Pastures wrapped him in.

Yet it had to be done now, lest the venture should wreck itself upon the rock which this pub door symbolised. Sweating, despite the cold air, as others pushed past to enter.

'How will ah know him,' he'd demanded of Ike, back there where he belonged. 'What's he like?'

'Fast women,' had been the sneer. Making Sam squirm before finally advising him to look for this 'big thin bloke wearing t'best overcoat in theer'. Telling him then to sod off before those ugly women needed another drink.

Sam hadn't got very far inside the pub. The act of going through the door had reduced him to trembling as the crush met him, a barrier of men, many in uniform, pressing close to highly made-up women, their hair expensively styled in high waves above shoulder-padded costumes that never saw the light of day in poorer quarters. Thick cigarette clouds were blown from painted mouths as they laughed and chatted, pencilled eye-brows lifting as they spoke. Their air of independence and unconcern, and the manner in which they laughed away the touching hands created in Sam a disbelief. They had pushed him, this crowd. Sending him all ways in their clumsiness, not caring in their own pursuit of enjoyment. Forgetting the war for a while. For here were the spenders, not the working people that he knew and felt comfortable with. These were people used to having money, used to having the things it could buy, surrounded by the slime which such style attracts. And Sam didn't like being there.

He'd finally reached the crowded bar, literally elbowing and shoving his way through them. Conscious of the sneering looks which his poor clothing attracted from those past whom he'd wriggled. Having to repeat his order for a mere gill of beer half-a-dozen times, whilst being ignored in favour of those asking behind him for more expensive drinks. Glaring in the most warlike manner he could muster at this youngish barmaid who smiled and bantered with those who freely tipped her. Making him wait until they did not need her before finally relenting to serve him. Snatching up his shilling and coldly eyeing him as he took his change and dared to speak.

'Ah'm looking for Chucky Morris,' he'd said, pocketing the coppers and grimacing at the first taste of the beer. 'Ah've come all way up from Attercliffe to see him'.

She hadn't been impressed, and made it plain. 'So what? Ah come all way down from Millhouses every neet, even in t'blitz.'

He'd scowled over his glass at that. She reminded him of Rosy Crapper back home. All mouth and no respect. So he'd sniffed, trying hard to promote an air of confidence. Getting only another hostile glare as she'd moved on, suddenly smiling as yet another hand waved yet another pound note. Leaving him to fume and scan around, looking to see the best top coat.

His efforts in this had been constantly obstructed by others, despite him craning his neck and lifting himself aloft on stretched toes. He tried for all his worth not to overbalance and fall against those around him, wishing they would part to clear his view, or at least have the decency to ask his purpose and thereby point out his target for tonight.

Until, glory of glories, he'd seen him. The one he knew and felt had to be him. Chucky the spiv, with the slicked, oiled hair set in raised ridges reaching back from his forehead. The sharp featured face that lacked any softness in the eyes, one that would forever remind our lad of the night that he stepped inside the underworld.

He was there, and Sam had stood panic-stricken for a while, just watching him. Pushing the barrel glass he held in heavy ringed fingers repeatedly forward as though to prove a point in the conversation taking place with his thick-set broken-nosed partner. The shining whiteness of a beautifully laundered shirt with dazzling cuff links at the wrists was matched by a sparkling pin holding down his pearl grey tie. Cutting a figure that cried out its expensiveness. Finished off by a black Crombie overcoat.

'Aye, aye,' thinks Sammy. 'Ah'm in'. An approach admirable in its daring considering his size, his dearth of funds, and the quality of the opposition. Although I always saw such bravery on his part as being confirmation of his misplaced belief that he could do owt and get away with it. Still, as I said, there's this

Chucky character no more than six foot away, with our lad waiting for one leg to stop twitching before moving in for the kill. Beset by two voices within, one urging him to make his move as the other bade him caution. Leaving him as usual in the panic of indecision which always culminated in an explosion of action or words outside of his own control. As it did here. Because, not really understanding how, emotion suddenly drove him forward to close the gap. And he'd found himself twisting his fat little neck back to peer under his cap at these two villains, loudly demanding of one if he was the person needed. Or as he put it, 'Hey up pal. Are tha' Chucky Morris? Is it thee wot can get owt?'

Now Chucky – to his credit – had remained calm. Icy calm. Choosing instead to slowly hover his furious gaze until it rested fully upon the rain-coated, flat-capped, podgy little thing now placed between him and his equally white-faced cohort.

'Who,' he'd said, keeping his voice low, though filled with menace, 'the twatting hell are you?'

Sam had eased back the cap from his sweating forehead, committed now to getting his purpose known. Not realising how loud was his nerve-wracked voice as he told of his belief that Chucky was involved in such things, of his wife's desire and how he'd paid the fare all the way from Attercliffe.

All of this had poured from him as he conquered the fear that had held him from the moment Edna had fired him with the daring of it. Cascading words upon the transfixed pair before him in a torrent of decibels that grew higher with each passing moment. Until he was virtually screaming before a now almost silent pub, into Chucky's bog-eyed face.

Now it was the spiv's turn to start trembling with a fear born of the fact that this unknown maniac could get him sent down for ten years whilst his evil-looking mate was having none of it, spinning on his heel and barging out, no doubt anxious to create space should there by chance be any plain-clothes police in that night.

Chucky had found himself unable to speak. Save for clapping a hand across this gibbering midget's mouth, he was powerless to stem the tide of incrimination that washed over him. He failed to see the humour in Sam's hysterical laugh at his wife's unusual want, and his joke about her thinking that 'they just grow on trees,' remaining silent, with a fury which caused twin purple spots to appear on both cheeks. Sam took this silence to mean his request was being considered, and so pressed on with it. Making things worse.

'Everybody down our end talks about thee, tha knows,' Sam had chortled loudly. 'Her next door told us – and thi mate Ike – tha knows who ah mean, Ike Mosely, reight robbing cow, him. Mind thee, their old lass and her mother are t'same'. Sam drained the remaining dregs of his glass to lubricate his over-worked throat. Nervous again as the spiv hissed to follow him, copying his departed mate's style to force his way out past the shocked onlookers, not used to such matters being so openly discussed. Followed in his wake by a Sam desperately trying not to lose him again, flushed by the false belief that his pleas were about to be granted, quite unaware of the effect he had generated by them. Out again into that cold night air, pleading once more to the back of Chucky's figure of how he 'ampt got much left now, tha knows, so don't sell us a bunch. She only wants one'.

He found himself seized by his front, and slammed against a wall in the darkness. His cap lifted at the front by the pressure applied, finally silencing him. Listening to a voice shaking with anger as Chucky explained the possible damage he had caused. Of how he needed a publicity agent like he needed afternoon tea with the

One of the main focal points of Sheffield was Fitzalan Square, with the statue of King Edward VII, in the late 1930's

Chief Constable, only in a much more obscene way. Our lad had closed his eyes as for a heart-stopping moment he'd believed that the clenched fist inches from his mouth was about to be applied, emphasising the spiv's point of how loose talk could easily lead to his having to trade in his expensive tastes for those of a more austere prison nature.

Thankfully, and no doubt influenced by Sam's legs buckling and the way in which he was now having to hold him up, Chucky had resisted the urge to mete out revenge, preferring instead to wrench off Sam's beloved best cap. And with one violent sweep had sent it soaring up and outward from them, flying away in a graceful arc above the deserted silent stalls of the rag market behind, bringing forth from our lad a painful moan at such loss. Despite the thought of the eight shillings and eleven

pence invested in it, and the knowledge that his other one had a cigarette burn in the top, he had not complained, prudence for once telling him that only his cowering posture was saving him from painful retribution.

Slowly the tension had eased, as Chucky now chose to lecture him on his foolishness with words. Scaring our lad with warnings of the dangers involved in such dealings, leading him on to believe that the spiv might yet overlook his stupidity and help him, a false hope which once again triggered off a nervous stream of dialogue from Sam about his need.

One that the spiv this time reacted quickly to by once again slamming Sam back, making him squeal as his head met the brick and promising that should our lad ever set foot inside his pub again to pester him, his departed mate would seek him out. Spelling out the barbarous taste of crippling injury to be inflicted with such clarity that Sam had broken wind in fear of it, nullifying any further need for Chucky to carry on.

The spiv had then stepped back, and staring intently into our lad's petrified face had asked for payment. Making Sam frantically drag what money he possessed from his pocket, doing his best to count in the pale light of a nearby gas lamp.

'Ah've got nine-and-fourpence left,' he'd said, correcting the sum quickly by explaining that he needed threepence of that for his tram fare back.

'Gimme that nine bob,' he was told. And he had, heart sinking as it disappeared, trying not to think of it as instructions were passed for the deal to take place, nodding all the time as he was fed lurid details of the risk he was taking. Of police and prisons and courts who would all have their share of him were he not silent and careful. Of how he should now depart this place, to wait beneath the grim imposing statue of Edward the Seventh that dominated Fitzalan Square above them. To wait for a man called Joe who would come to him, bearing the fruit.

The promises were accompanied by a shove as the spiv had done with him, eager to be rid, only pausing to answer Sam's frantic request of how he would know this messenger.

'Don't worry, tha'll know him' was the answer. 'Just watch for somebody wi' a big limp. If it's not Joe hiding a coconut it'll be somebody else wi' a bad rupture.'

Now Fitzalan Square in those days was something of a focal point in town, being used by thousands as a meeting place, as was Coles Corner at the other end of High Street. It was also well served by public toilets, so that for one reason or another there was always a steady flow in and around it. This being so, such a popular venue naturally attracted its fair share of the male sex who were judged to be 'different', something which regular users of the place were well aware of and therefore prepared to be cautious about. Which was fine, if you knew. But if you didn't, well, you'd quickly find yourself surprised at the number of unknown persons suddenly anxious to know more about you. Which is where our lad comes in again.

'Cos there he is, waiting for his coconut under the King, with hands inside raincoat pockets and cap pulled well down. Convinced that every copper in town is watching him, and trying to look law-abiding by silently whistling to keep his spirits up, when up steps this well-dressed sort, giving him a warm smile.

'Aye aye,' thinks Sammy. 'It's him, Joe, wi' me stuff.' So he smiles back. And the toff, encouraged by this, moves to stage two by bidding him 'Hello'. This friendliness sucked our lad into believing that he's the man. Though he couldn't fathom out where the coconut could be hidden, seeing as he hadn't noticed any unusual bulges anywhere. Or a limp.

So he takes the final plunge, anxious to be gone, by saying, 'Ah'm glad that tha's come. Ah've been waiting for thi'. An observation which turned the other feller's smile into a positive beam, spreading to light up the whole of his face when Sam innocently hit him with the next one of, 'has tha brought me a little treat?'

Now that one just about flattened him. I mean it was obviously not his first excursion to Cleethorpes, and no doubt he'd come across some in a hurry. But the speed that Sam was working at took even him by surprise. Making him clear his throat and bend forward to whisper that there were better places to be. Bringing out a puzzled 'what for?' as Sam did his best to conclude his business and catch his tram. This stranger reminded Sam that what they were about to do was illegal, an act which, if caught, would almost certainly result in going to prison. Sam understood and nodded too, so that when the toff then suggested they should go to his car nearby our lad's eyes were like bin lids.

'Car? Tha's brought it in a car? Bleeding hell, how big is it? Ah've got to go back on a tram, tha knows.' All of which had his new friend non-plussed.

'Tram? Get what on a tram?'

'Me coconut,' our lad had burst out, exasperated by all of this.

'Coconut? I haven't any coconuts,' he was told, the pair of them now looking lost by all of this.

'Tha must 'ave,' Sam insisted. 'Ah've paid thi mate nine bob for one. He said Joe'd bring it. That's thee, innit?'

'No.'

'Well, who the bleeding hell are tha?' he'd demanded, his voice once again rising to alarm the other and make passers-by stare.

'It doesn't matter, doesn't matter,' the man had said, turning now to leave quickly. His pace increased as Sam pursued, still shouting his demands for goods he knew nothing of. The pair of 'em breaking into a full trot, dodging in and out, one seeking to shake off the other, until, catching one foot on the bottom memorial step Sam had crashed forward, smashing a knee into its unforgiving hardness. Above him, the monarch cared little for his plight, not letting Sam's curses disturb him from surveying this dirty little square of his realm.

The curses of a lad cheated and robbed were carried on a cold wind back to Attercliffe, unheard above the noise and merriment of Chucky's pub.

The last Green Bottle

Views like this burned themselves into my memory as a kid. This is Brightside Lane, with English Steel's River Don Works in the background.

MY ARRIVAL IN ATTERCLIFFE in 1935 was somewhat overshadowed by other wide-ranging events of that year.

For one thing Sheffield Wednesday beat West Bromwich Albion at Wembley to win the F.A. Cup, something they have never managed since, thereby creating a level of anticipation amongst their supporters to reach the proportions of sighting Haley's Comet.

It was also the year that the driving test became compulsory for those wealthy enough to buy a car. A piece of legislation hardly designed to throw the workless East End into a panic, seeing as the average manual wage, even if you had a job, only ran to two hundred and thirty-five quid a year or less than a fiver each week, hardly the sort of income to go test-driving a new motor, eh?

And, although the only earth tremors we ever felt were more from the heavy presses than the earth's crust moving, Mr Richter invented his famous scale. Not that it mattered, queuing outside a pawnshop, but I thought I'd just mention it.

So that if you should ask me today to recall things from then, none of the above would get a mention. Because to me they're not important to the time. Not like the big chimneys were, those huge stacks that announced the presence of Firth Browns, English Steel, Brown Baileys, Edgar Allens, Hadfields and many more. Monstrous things, towering like brick-built flags and silently shaping our skyline. Man-made giants that spent their lives throwing out furls of stinging black smoke. Lords of the vast works and huddled houses making up their realm. Scattering aloft their bitter harvest of filth to form dark clouds sitting in permanence above.

An ugly presence, lacking nature's rain. Filled instead with this acrid compost of burnt waste thrown high by the heavy plant that we dwelt amongst. A tainted gift. Showered upon us from their blackened mouths and born of the awesome heat of roaring industrial bellies.

Funnelled aloft through these high lungs which brushed the sky, taking out the shining sun, leaving us instead a legacy of gloom, so that we too were grey with a tasteless wine of poor air that turned faces pallid deep down in the forest of tall chimneys.

Not now, though. Not now that they've all been felled. Collapsing by number to the woodsmen of progress and change and economics, that three-bladed axe brought in to cull them with neither pity nor thought for whatever significance they carried for us. Slain by those not seeing those high ambassadors of our prosperity with the eyes of we who were born here.

Smoking envoys announcing our industry with their dirty pictures, that spelled out the overflowing order books for our steel and its forging, a bedrock of endless work which we took for granted. Formed through long years stretching back to before my time, so that we, as kids, grew up on it, having no knowledge of being without work or the lack of a regular wage, accustomed by habit to starting a day with the clarion sounds of hooters calling the faithful to gainful prayer.

Each one distinct by note or duration from the others, telling those of us living in the citadel, of its place in our lives and whether a shift was about to begin . . . or end. Raucous outside alarms that we didn't need to set, ingraining us to an extent that not even removal to far-off estates could erase, finding such un-accustomed silence impossible to sleep with, and perversely we missed that which before we had sleepily cursed on icy mornings.

A nuisance now remembered only by those who lived with them, amongst those tall chimneys.

Yet I wouldn't want such thoughts to be seen as grieving their passing. Not when you recall the mutilation which they heaped upon our environment. Any remorse over their death can only be in the way in which it took so many livelihoods with it. It is much better now to talk of other things of then, which do not leave the same bitter taste.

Like apple cores, for instance. The way we kids would fight over them has to be a burning memory for anyone my age. How we would stick like the proverbial glue to a pal who might be good enough to offer you his. Once he had finished with it, that is.

I've lost count of the times I waited for one, warding off any outside attempt at usurping my first claim to it. Watching and waiting patiently as my benefactor slobbered away through the body of it with great crunching bites, unintentionally creating for me this aching salivaral tingle all around my gums in my anticipation of such sweetness. The pleasure of his leavings. If he kept his promise, that is.

Oh, I had my share of those, I can tell you. We all did. Never once letting the noisy distasteful sight of another mouth feasting first lessen our desire for it. Except, that is, unless it was one of snotty Pete Fairfax's. There was never a queue for his. Not with his awful nasal predicament. Even I drew a line at that.

Consequently Pete was the only kid we knew who had to literally beg us to take what in other circumstances we fought over.

'Ennyonyer wandiscore?' he would plead as we'd all turn away. He never managed to quite comprehend our distorted features at the mere thought of it.

And I can also look back fondly on the wonderful collection of marbles I amassed, the ones I kept surreptitiously hidden in a white flour bag beneath the old shoes in a bottom cupboard. Not so much to guard against theft, but rather as a way of ensuring that no-one else could handle their beauty. Treasured orbs of glass, lovingly counted each day and individually known to me despite any difference in their make-up.

Reds and blues, greens and browns and yellows. Colour masses, often broken by curling shafts of white or other hues trapped within, making them a thing to desire in their glorious combinations of prettiness. Ones I found unable to resist the touch of, rolling their smoothness in and around my fingers, expressing my collective love for them, I found myself unable to resist the touch of them.

Yet still isolating some to be my favourites by their specialness of reflection, or their triumphs in arenas formed by the metal gridded grates which covered drain-pipes in the school yard. Or within the bounds of chalk circles crudely drawn on the flagstones of a cold street.

We developed to a fine art that skill of firing them from between a cocked thumb and forefinger, catapulting to defeat an opponent's champion with velocities measured by 'Tibs', or full and half 'Scutches'. Terms of engagement brought to bear in street battles, claiming by conquest yet another precious 'Mab'.

That was something that I must have been fairly proficient in, seeing as my flour bag held over eighty of them before the fever of winning left me, most of them earned by kneeling on hard surfaces that left my knuckles red raw with the soreness of taking on those who would have mine, along with the cheats who sought a joust by using ugly steel ball bearings when all of their mabs had been lost. A cowardly thing to do, I thought.

Almost to the level of shame reached by pitiful souls reduced to begging a game with their detestable 'stonks'. Those pathetic, inferior, substitutes for the real thing made from some obscure dark compound which split asunder on the first scutch. Paste fakes, only to be considered for combat if a real match was unavailable, as a knight might see a contest with some peasant. Such then was our passion for this old street game, played with an intensity our teachers would have drooled over had it been applied to 'doing us sums'.

That's a comparison which in retrospect I see the sense of. But not then. Not while-ever the chance to be champion remained. Even against a set of stonks.

Anyway, I grew out of it, swapping all of my hard-fought-for collection one day for Tommy Jessop's front bicycle lamp. One of those Ever Ready type that held a double battery which you could warm up in the oven to get a bit more life out of. Before moving on to my next all-consuming involvement . . . rabbits.

I've lost count of all the Saturdays I spent surrounded by these loveable pets in that archway on the edge of the old rag market down Dixon Lane. Living hordes of them there were, hopping about in straw-lined cages that separated them by size or breed, with prices starting from half-a-crown.

I sat hours in that cavern sometimes, taking in the smell of it all, with six-week-old puppy dogs yapping loud enough to drown the throaty noises of pigeons stacked above them in boxes. Looking down on me as I'd bend to gently stroke the bony backs of bright yellow

day-old chicks, craftily left in the doorway, inside an open wooded frame that passing kids could not resist begging their parents to buy from. At a tanner each.

And there were times when I too succumbed, taking them home in the cardboard box supplied. One with air holes in the lid, making me fidget on the top deck of the tram with their continuous cheeping which could get you thrown off.

Minuscule living things that wobbled on legs like cotton thread and which we sought to keep alive with breadcrumbs and water. Leaving them at bedtime in the fire's hearth to gain the dying heat, hoping to find them still alive the following cold morning, to get one more day from them. But they never did. And we'd throw their lifeless bodies in the bin outside, their short-lived pleasure done with, wishing then that we'd spent the money on 'spice' instead.

Not like rabbits. The ones I bought and earned from doing a paper round. They were the ones to excite me, except, that is, for the lone time when for some unknown reason I deviated and bought two pigeons

Chimneys towering over a smokey central Sheffield, looking across Commercial Street towards Neepsend. The Town Hall tower is to the left of the photo.

instead. Don't ask me why, because my association with this pair didn't last more than three hours. And that includes getting them home.

To be honest, it was a barmy thing to do, buying them. I hadn't the first idea of how to look after them and, worse still, not even anywhere to keep them. Soft sod that I was, I just did it. On the spur, so to speak, and I remember breathing with relief at finding nobody home when I got there with them. Creeping in to sit on our settee with this brown-paper carrier bag on my knees, and these two wriggling about in the bottom of it. Nervously opening the top to peer in at them, not prepared for this great . . . whoosh.

And one of the buggers comes shooting out before I can do owt, making me yell out and jump up, dropping the bag and setting the other one free as well. With the pair of them now doing aerial manoeuvres through the house and kitchen, landing where they liked, and me like a chuff making pigeon sounds, trying to tempt them back into the bag.

'Til the back door flew open, and me Mam walked in, carrying a load of shopping which she promptly dropped with a loud shriek as one of my new friends dive-bombed her on the way out, with me following it before she could gather the gist of all this.

It was hours later before I dared return that day. And I copped it when I did, for the bird still in there when I'd run off had shat the full length of our sideboard, including all over the face of the chiming clock she was still paying a Banner's cheque off for. Then, having no doubt an immense sense of fun, it had decided to take up residence in the big light bowl hanging from our ceiling. And she'd had to turn both bulbs on in broad daylight to burn the awkward sod out again. She finally got rid of it through the back door with wild swipes of a towel that had sent one of her best silver vases flying and

put a big dent in it.

I didn't bother with pigeons again after that. I stuck to rabbits, mainly on the principle that I was in no rush to sample me Mam's enthusiasm for pointing out the shortfalls of owning pigeons.

Mind you, I did have a few dogs. And there was one time I was talked into keeping a bantam cock, which was lovely, until some rotten sod came one night and introduced their cat to it.

So, it was mainly rabbits for me, kept in rough hutches I made by scrounging old orange boxes from the shops. Knocked together with nails three times too big and door hinges fashioned from leather cut out of old shoe soles.

Yes . . . I had this well-remembered way of making do and mending when it came to keeping rabbits as a kid, loving and cosseting them all on thick beds of straw bought for ninepence a bag. There was a docile black and white Dutch, alongside the more lively chinchilla grey English buck. There was my beautiful Angora, whose pure white pelt was brilliantly offset by its blood red eyes. And, most impressive of all, my Flemish giant.

It was a huge thing to have, so large in itself that I had to sell two of my Dutch to give him a hutch of his own. My pride and joy. Getting the lion's share of everything in the way of greens I could beg, along with this magical elixir recommended to me whereby you mixed old tea leaves in with his bran.

God knows who first thought of that, but I'll tell you what. They loved it. It made their eyes bright, their pelts thick . . . and fit? Well, to give you some idea of its effect on them, I once took this big Flemish to Herbert Lee's when he asked me to mate it with a coal black English doe he'd got. And the pair of us had to sit on his hutch when it got in there to stop it falling off the house bricks it was resting on.

Brightside Lane in the 1950's – a working street which saw a twice-daily ebb and flow of shift workers, as well as regular flooding.

All you could hear and see of his were these squeals from its little black face sticking out from under what looked like a big grey blanket covering it. And, to Herbert's deep alarm, the wire netting started to come away from the front as the huge head of my rampant beast slammed against it with regular thumps.

Anyway, Herbert panicked and between us we dragged mine out before he killed the poor little sod, leaving me with a right old job of taking him back home in disgrace. And that was no picnic either with him still in an unbridled state of arousal.

My arms fair ached trying to hold him to me with his body stiff and jerking and his long back legs raking me to death down the front. He ripped all of my jumper, got through my shirt, and left me with scratches that deep you could have put a zip on them. In fact, I had to miss the school's swimming lesson that week when our teacher saw them. That's how sore and ugly they looked.

I was mad about that, and never let him out again.

Wonderful memories now. Ones kept locked away, waiting for the right time to look at them again. A personal album of fading pictures showing places and faces from yesteryear, now turning sepia with age, putting into perspective today's fallacy that modern comfort automatically equals a better life.

Not in my book it doesn't. It simply removes ancient hardships . . . that's all. Or ancient blessings, which then we didn't appreciate.

The spirit of wartime and the days of leaving doors unlocked. A natural breeding ground for short tempers and beer-filled bust-ups made worse by the failing of letting the rules slip. No, it isn't better now in that respect, for ours was a growing-up time of laughter at childish games and pranks, followed by the tears of punishment when things went too far. Teaching us to know right from wrong, administered by parents determined to show that there is a price to pay for everything in this life. I remember that well. And I wouldn't have swapped that lesson for one of King George's overcoats.

I wouldn't swap the memory either of that day our gang set off on a tram to Vulcan Road to spend the afternoon playing on the canal bank at Tinsley Locks. When we'd all raced up the stairs to sit in that big front bay to get a good view over the works' walls. Noisy as hell, with snotty Pete making a racket by sliding the irons of his brand new clogs over those metal studs they set in the aisle for extra grip when the tram swayed about. Anyway, as usual, we'd left getting up to leave until the last second. Perhaps no more than fifty yards from our stop, we all made this mad dash back to the stairs, pushing and pulling to be the first off. It was won by Pete, determined to hold the rest of us up on the way down.

Now you'll recall that those iron stairs were very steep as well as twisted. Treacherous to say the least, even when taking your time. So that when this hand came over my head to grab and yank Pete back, I had a ring-side view of the lad's steel-shod feet shooting out before him as he slipped. And he went the rest of the way down like a lance, planting them with a sickening thud into the centre top of this poor conductor's back.

Well . . . his wooden ticket holder shot off the tram, he went full length inside the bottom deck and I'm left looking in awe at a dent in his peaked hat that hadn't been there when he clocked on that day. Because, being second down the stairs, I'd landed on it.

No word of a lie, but the rest of us literally trampled over the conductor's legs, diving off in un-adulterated panic at what Pete had just done. And my last recall of this is haring over the bridge on legs I couldn't feel.

Sadly, Pete never made it with us. Having bashed his knee falling down those stairs, and giving the passengers time to grab him, this whole sorry episode ended with him being dragged by the collar to those tram sheds at Weedon Street, getting regular clips around his crying head by a rather miffed conductor using a damaged hat.

Anyway, they took his name and address and told him his Dad would be hearing about it. Then threw him out to limp back home. Alone. And knowing him I bet he hoped and prayed that it was all an idle threat to frighten his senses. That he'd be spared a meeting with his Dad's belt.

All the Dads did that then, you see. Use a belt, I mean. Well, all of them that I knew did, seeing it as a sort of early day nuclear deterrent. And whereas now missiles are shaped like a tube with an explosive cone on the end, ours were made from broad leather. With a big brass buckle instead. One that went off with just as big a bang when it landed.

There was no three-minute warning with it, either, just this flash as it was launched from around his beer belly. That's when you dived for cover, hoping it would miss. Only it rarely did, and the fall-out from it was bloody painful. Every house had their own rocket. And I can promise you that I personally would have preferred two pastings from me Mam to one of his.

For she put more faith into her flat hand. Not that it was a piece of cake getting it, mind you. Far from it. I mean, you have to take into account that her palm would be hardened from years of turning a mangle, as well as pummelling wet clothes on a rubbing board. So when she connected, your flesh had a habit of turning a deep red and convincing you that a bare bone was now showing. And there'd be no hiding place from her either, once she began. Whether you dived under a table, behind a chair, or tried barricading a bedroom door. I know . . . I tried them all.

There was even one time when I shot between her legs and locked my arms around her knees to stop her moving, thinking she'd be too scared to hit me in case she over-balanced.

Fat chance. All it took was a handful of hair as she reached down behind her and then I was wide open as she cocked her leg over me. I paid extra for that one for trying to fool her.

What got me about this practice, though, was the daft dialogue they always used to accompany it. Such as, 'Tha's been asking for this,' when I had done no such thing. Not verbally anyway.

And when she came out with the next one of, 'Does tha want another 'un?' you became positive that here was someone whose anger had hi-jacked her brain. I mean, I'd be there in a crouched position with both arms over my head and screaming the place down. Does that sound like someone anxious to carry on?

Had it been a bag of midget gems on offer, then no doubt I'd have snatched her hand off. But more pain? Naturally you said, 'No'. Loud and tearfully. Only to be amazed that such honesty then acted as a spur to give you more cosh on the grounds of how she'd be 'bleeding sick of doing this'.

And I, reeling from the effects, would silently muse that in which case she should definitely 'stop doing it then, you silly mare'. Not that I would have dared to say such a thing, I dread to think how many days I'd have been off school had I done so.

Better instead to follow the two golden rules you needed to survive a good pasting from your Mam. One .

. . put her off stroke by continual movement and yelling loud enough for them next door to hear. And two . . . never laugh at what her temper led her into saying.

For this well-versed opera made sense to her, and experience taught that not singing the same song only added more power to her repertoire, as those of you who were around at the time will know if your mother was as adept at laying it on as mine was. Your head will still have these funny little ridges in it that get in the way of a comb.

Well, it's a long time now. And I can safely look back to when I paid for breaking the rules, seeing now what I couldn't then, that she was just as big a victim in applying it as I was being on the receiving end. It was the way of things, and I'm convinced that I came to no lasting harm from it. It kept us in line, and if I have any more to add then it must be the thought that it's a good job we didn't have soft social workers interfering with their traditional way of correcting us. 'Cos me Mam would have poshed them and all. Especially if they'd been daft enough to laugh at her.

We still took the chances, though, despite the inevitability of such retribution. As kids always will. Although I will say that our type of nuisance never reached today's liberal attitude of giving them freedom to destroy and intimidate the old.

Ours was tempered by a dread of being caught, backed up with solid clouts of a bobby's cape. All the same, we had our fun. And there were times later, having left home, when I'd lay on that army bed penniless on long duty-free Sundays and think of them.

Homesick for familiar places, with clear mental pictures of us all 'scroaming' over high back walls in the winter darkness. With the sharp edges of old bricks cutting bare knees in the whispered race not to be last over. Dropping down into the black pit of an unknown yard, then regretting such bravado as we ran from the noise clutching a bleeding wound.

Scars to prove we dared, and lucky they were not worse from the stupid game of dodging across trams bearing down hard on us. Testing your nerve, with the dubious prize being the furious clanging of a white-faced driver's foot-bell. Cursing us for the lack of sense we obviously suffered from, yet unable to chase our laughing retreat. So we'd roam boring streets to shin fluted gas lamps and swing Tarzan-like on their shaking arms. Copying his ridiculous call as we swang legs aloft to hook alongside a tenuous grip. Hanging head down over worn flagstones, impressing watching girls with this practised bravery.

The grubby earth of a canal bank would form an arena for laughing bouts of wrestling which occasionally would transcend the realms of accepted play. Leading to a fight which always ending with the tearful loser saying 'Hen' to his straddling victor's crowing of a loud 'Cock'.

A penance demanded in such matters then. And not a pleasant way to concede with your face buried in the crotch of the tatty trousers squatting over it. Looked down on by a grinning crowd who circled in excited judgement of your efforts to free arms pinned back behind your head, held firm by he who had licked you. And having got such yield he would then rise to strut around, rolling down sleeves pushed back to the elbow for the battle. So that you rose alone, eyes downcast, without the offer of a token hand in respect for your efforts in the contest. Silently assessing him as a lucky bastard for winning.

There were a few of those for me, I can tell you. Just as I can tell you of my excitement at getting my first long trousers.

A coming of age mark, agreed by all parents as signifying that childhood was over. That you were now a lad, big enough to wear them. Putting an end to those years of knees and thighs exposed to bitter winds painting them deep red with chap.

Worn till threadbare with patches as their daily saviour, especially on the bum where excessive ground contact took its toll. Running repairs not always blending harmoniously with the existing material. Leaving the wearer conspicuous by the parts he couldn't see.

As Harry Owen will know from the time he came to school wearing light grey ones strikingly complimented by a bright red blob strategically placed between his ample buttocks.

A crude attempt on his mother's part, we thought when first clapping eyes on it. One to give an impression of his arse being extremely sore, made worse still by the way in which this half-inch broad badge disappeared and came out again as he walked.

Like a flashing beacon it was, one for us all to follow. Cut, we later found, from the body warming coat of a greyhound their old feller earned extra cash from by exercising it for the owner.

A poor choice, fascinating us by the way it seemed to wink. Making Harry cringe and blush and clamp a hand over it, not knowing which way to turn as we'd followed him in a column, singing to the tune of Snow White's dwarves a made-up ditty of:

'Aye 'O . . . aye 'o . . . don't let thi patches show
Tha'll never be a scout with thi arse hanging out
Aye 'O . . . aye 'O . . . Aye 'O,'

. . . over and over again, until the bell had rung. Breaking the fun.

He'd fled home at that. Missing lessons for a wailing protest to a bemused Mam over the way she had cast his patched-up fate into our eager hands. Pleading relief by way of a better choice of colour to his rear end and returning after dinner with the red flag now replaced with a dark grey check one, cut from a cap left over from when his grand-dad died. Looking more presentable to us, but not to Mr Langston, who promptly caned him for leaving school without permission.

A hard man to cross, not one to listen to excuses of how we had persecuted the lad over his Mam's atrocious needlework.

And having no legal reason for 'wagging it' Harry held out a trembling hand. The punishment was doubled by having his name removed from the milk monitor's list for a month as an expression of his disapproval.

I remembered that years later. Trying to realise a cretinous corporal's dream of making my boot caps gleam to perfection by making us rub endless circles of polish over them. Driving you mad with such enforced bullshit. Letting that picture of Harry take its place, and the way he had avoided us after the caning.

A hurt gesture of annoyance for us that hadn't lasted long. It never did with him, not having the nature to be left out from us. And it took only a sharp threat of chucking him out of the gang to end his sulking nonsense, bringing him back to heel.

And I thought of that later, along with the strokes he suffered because of it.

Like the time he got a new snake belt for his birthday. And me, without one as usual, being filled with this unfair urge to take it from him.

You see, snake belts were all the rage with us then, making our old fashioned braces obsolete, even the Mickey Mouse ones. And seeing as how Harry was a softer touch than Madge Dunlop's left breast I went all out for it.

I could just imagine its beautiful lateral stripes of blue and gold holding my scruffy short trousers up. With that silver 'S' shaped hook at the front drawing everyone's attention.

It was, I thought, the ultimate item for a dull image. One to pull the birds if ever I saw it.

Better than a big quiff you could shape in the front of your hair by caking it in lard. Or long grey clean socks that held themselves up without a white elastic garter.

Better even than Jack Whitely's multi-coloured sleeveless Fair Isle jumper . . . when he wore it.

And I wanted it. 'Cos we couldn't afford one at our house.

Anyhow, I'm there with eyes like balm cakes homing in like that Flemish buck rabbit. Trying the old opening ploy of asking him to let me try it on for him, only to be astonished and disgusted by the awkward sod refusing to fall for it.

I mean, conning Harry had always been on the level of pinching a babby's dummy, until now that is. He just wouldn't budge.

So I tried plan 'B'. Which was to offer him the bargain swap of my well-thumbed *Film Fun* annual, circa 1948. Getting from him in return a snort that would have sent the tail of Tommy Nesbitt's ragcart pony soaring high in expectancy.

Now, to be honest, I'd expected this from him because he'd already owned this book once before. 'Cos I remembered him trading it to Gordon Lamb for two trolley wheels. And he in turn had swapped it to me for a kaleidoscope tube that I'd given Herbert Lee a six-by-eight photo of Roy Rogers for.

Well you did that then, see. Even if it sounds complicated. It was the only way you got owt. Except for Christmas and birthdays, if you were lucky.

We swapped, then went about pretending it was new.

But, that aside, I battled all day for that belt and got nowt. So I left him alone to stew in his own meanness till the following day's playtime.

Then I cornered him, and this time did away with all nonsense by demanding his price for it. Fed up of watching him parade around, showing off to the lasses, without a jumper on, even though he shook with the cold.

Only to stagger back, losing what bit of colour I had when he named it. My incomparable A.J.S. motor bike tyre. Now I know it sounds daft today with kids pushing buttons for fun, but we all pushed tyres.

In fact a top-class tyre did for our street 'cred' then what knowing how to by-pass a burglar alarm does now. You were a top man with a racing tyre, anything less was looked on as being deprived, even by our standards. We burnt the streets up hitting them with a stick, and anybody without had to run alongside asking for a go.

And we did hit 'em. We made them fly, guiding them with deft touches, although you sometimes lost them with devastating results.

As Sammy Gregory did when his Wolsey Eight model shot across Staniforth Road, knocking flat a telegram boy off of his red Post Office bike, before bouncing up to hit this bloke on the back of his neck who'd bent down to miss it.

Talk about run for it.

As I said, you had to be good with 'em. Especially a thoroughbred like mine. One with a surface span no more than four inches across. Built for a speed to leave them dead. Perfect response, cornering on less than an inch of tread. A glorious moon rocket amongst steam rollers, giving me endless pride and pleasure by creating a slipstream to blast laggards with their heavy-duty rubbish scrounged from tips. Or the murky waters of the canal.

A jaguar amongst donkeys. One I was loathe to trade. Especially to a fat sod with a snake belt who would never realise its full potential for speed.

But trade I did. Reluctantly. Allowing visions of that new belt strapped around me to overcome any further need to prove further its pedigree.

Ignoring the disbelief of others for doing it, as well as Harry's excitement at getting it. Waving disdainfully aside the objectionable offer of his own tyre as a substitute. Seeing it as a brutish thing, worn through in parts to its canvas inner, ugly by its bulk and notorious for being sluggish to start.

Yet, sadly for me, it proved to be little more than a brief mirage. When, as I'd always known he would, Harry returned to reclaim it, driven out by a screaming mother when he'd gone home pushing my tyre with one hand, holding up his beltless kecks with the other. Shattering the illusion I had bathed in viewing its feel around me from the angles of a three-mirrored dressing table.

A cloud nine which burst in less than one hour with a shout for me to bring it down. And the sight of a tearful Harry under the impending threat of his Dad's leather friend.

I was left envying Harry's luck at having such a belt. And him to envy me racing my unbeatable A.J.S. My worn-out braces held up by a pin.

But that was a lifetime ago. And the tyre has now given way to a comfortable modern motor car. One having little need of the wooden peg previously used for guidance. Although I must say that the difference in running costs now does tend to spoil a pleasure I once got for nowt.

It's gone. As other things have. Those well-known city landmarks we always took our compass bearing from. Focal points like the *Empire*, the *Hippodrome* and the *Playhouse Theatre* in town.

Palaces of entertainment where for a blink in time we could shut away the greyness of our world with the colourful fantasy of theirs.

Only to rejoin it again amongst the heaving mass of an ancient rag market and the Fitzalan Square pubs of *The Bell* and *The Elephant*, ale houses that vied for the drinker's mantle of favouritism with *The Barleycorn*, *The Albert* and *The Pump* equally drawing us beyond the Moorhead monument. All viewed with disdain by the famous *Mucky Duck*.

Haunts that we reached on the familiar cream and blue colours of our buses and trams, a proud coat of arms resplendent upon their liveried sides.

Forming between them a superb, reliable and cheap transport system to leave other great cities weeping in envy. One that daily coped with the herculean task of carrying vast multitudes patiently awaiting them in the cold and rain, hoping the conductor would not shout 'full'.

Workers by the thousands, anxious to be home from a long day. To settle after tea beside a glowing coal fire, tuning in a valve-powered wireless to the microphonic voices of Ben Lyon and Bebe Daniels. Peter Brough educating his Archie, or Ted Ray in Variety Band Box holding up London's mighty traffic for *In Town Tonight*. Innocent programmes with squeaky clean scripts now butchered by the crude sword of puerile TV game shows.

Showering squealing contestants with sums of money that we wouldn't have seen for a year's work. What rubbish.

Well below that of our dear old Arthur Askey's daftness as he pranced around a piano on his toes, for all the world a big eyed sausage dog freaking out on a Bob Martins overdose as he warbled on about wanting to be a 'busy little bee'.

They don't make 'em like him anymore. And thinking back to how he performed I'm not surprised either.

Yet, for all of that, I'm still glad that I knew him. And all the rest of those radio stars. For they were the real England. The one where us kids were made to stand up for the old to sit down. Where sixty thousand could crush together at a football match without a single one getting his head kicked in. And little 'chavvy's' were passed overhead to the front by careful hands.

Where the only reference to race equality we ever heard was when the handicapper got his weights right at Doncaster, and left-handed people didn't scream about discrimination for being called 'dolly poshed'.

Where I was thrown out in disgrace from Jeannie Bolan's twelfth birthday party for trying to make them all laugh by reciting the nauseous rhyme of:

'Scattermatter custard. Green snot pie
Two dogs' giblets. One cat's eye
Stir it round until it's thick
Then swill it all down with a cup of cold sick'

. . . a joke which misfired badly. One of such poetic stupidity that even now, almost a half century later, I still cringe from the memory. As well as the sight of my choking hostess fleeing the room with a hand clamped to her mouth, followed by her mother. Oh well. At least I'd had my jelly and custard. And I could always plead in mitigation an ignorance due to a rough upbringing.

One that now, after a few pints, I often mourn the passing of. Perhaps from a sentimentality heavily laced by a concern of the speed at which so many birthdays have passed. Leaving me feeling alarmed at being surrounded by so many not old enough to remember the same things.